Baseball's Most
Wanted

D1044501

Also by Floyd Conner

Baseball's Most
Wanted

The Top 10 Book of the National Pastime's Outrageous Offenders, Lucky Bounces, and Other Oddities

Floyd Conner

Brassey's

WASHINGTON, D.C.

Copyright © 2000 Brassey's

Published in the United States by Brassey's. All rights
reserved. No part of this book may be reproduced in
any manner whatsoever without written permission from
the publisher, except in the case of brief quotations
embodied in critical articles and reviews.

Library of Congress Cataloging-in-Publication Data

Conner, Floyd, 1951–
   Baseball's most wanted : the top 10 book of the
national pastime's outrageous offenders, lucky bounces,
and other oddities / Floyd Conner.— 1st ed.
      p.   cm.
   Includes index.
   ISBN 1-57488-229-5
      1. Baseball players—Miscellanea.   I. Title

GV865 .A1 C63 2000
796.357'092'273—dc21
[B]
                                                    99-086476

Printed in Canada

Brassey's
22841 Quicksilver Drive
Dulles, Virginia 20166

Designed by Pen & Palette Unlimited

First Edition

10 9 8 7 6 5 4 3 2 1

Contents

Introduction

The 2000 season marks the 125th anniversary of major league baseball. During that time more than 15,000 players have appeared in the big leagues. Fewer than 200 of the game's immortals have been enshrined in the Baseball Hall of Fame. Their achievements are well known to any baseball fan. But what about all those other players?

Baseballs Most Wanted honors the game's most outrageous offenders. The book contains top ten lists of the worst hitters, wildest pitchers, and poorest fielders ever to play the game. The lists feature the unlikeliest heroes, most infamous goats, craziest fans, zaniest promotions, and the strangest things to occur during a game.

In today's market of high-priced free agents, pitcher Kevin Brown earns $15 million a year from the Los Angeles Dodgers. By contrast, Chicken Wolf, the lowest paid major leaguer ever under contract, was paid $9 a week to play for Louisville in 1882. Ten years later, Bumpus Jones pitched a no-hitter in his first major league game, and he wasn't even under contract. In 1899, a cigar store clerk, Eddie Kolb, actually gave the Cleveland Spiders a box of cigars for the privilege of pitching a major league game.

What do the following minor leaguers have in common? Joe Bauman set a professional baseball record by hitting seventy-two home runs in a season. Another slugger, Bob Crues, set another single season record by batting in 254 runs. Hector Espino set a minor league record with 484 career home runs. Bill Thomas won a record 383 games in his career. These minor league phenoms share one thing. None of them ever played in the major leagues.

In baseball almost anything can happen. The 1869 Cincinnati Red Stockings, baseball's first all professional team, had their 130-game undefeated streak snapped when an overzealous fan in Brooklyn jumped on the back of outfielder Cal McVey as he chased a fly ball. Another Cincinnati player, Edd Roush, was ejected from a game for falling asleep in the outfield. Dan Friend once played left field while dressed in a bathrobe. Manager Bobby Bragan entertained a crowd by performing a strip tease in the dugout.

Hall of Fame pitcher Jim Bunning, now a United States senator representing the commonwealth of

Kentucky, is not the only major league baseball player to go on to a successful career in politics. John Tener won twenty-five games in the majors and was later elected governor of Pennsylvania. Outfielder Fred Brown played in nine games with Boston at the turn of the century before turning to politics and serving terms as both governor and senator of the state of New Hampshire. After his playing days were over, pitcher Wilmer "Vinegar Bend" Mizell was a six-term congressman representing North Carolina. In his youth former New York Governor Mario Cuomo was an outstanding prospect in the Pittsburgh Pirates' organization. Future President Ronald Reagan was an announcer for the Chicago Cubs when he was discovered by Hollywood.

Some players just prefer carrying a big stick. Hack Miller, a .323 lifetime batter, used bats as heavy as sixty-five ounces. Another perennial .300 hitter, Bill "Little Eva" Lange, once brought a six-foot-long bat to the plate. On the other end of the scale, Eddie Gaedel, the smallest player in major league baseball history, also used the smallest bat, measuring a mere seventeen inches.

This book introduces you to nearly 700 of base-ball's most wanted players. Their offenses range from inept play to outrageous behavior. Be on the lookout for these individuals.

On the Dotted Line

Since the era of free agency began in the 1920s, baseball salaries have escalated rapidly. In 1999, the Los Angeles Dodgers signed ace right-hander Kevin Brown to a contract that will pay him $105 million over a seven-year period. By contrast, the entire payroll of the 1997 Pittsburgh Pirates totaled only $9 million. Players haven't always been so fortunate. Both Babe Ruth and Joe DiMaggio earned less than $1 million in their entire careers. The lowest paid player in baseball history was rookie Chicken Wolf, who earned $9 a week in 1882. Here are some of the most outrageous contracts in baseball history.

1. JOE BORDEN

Pitcher Joe Borden called himself Josephus the Phenomenal because of his extraordinary pitching. When the National League was founded in 1876, Borden was the winning pitcher in the first game. He also pitched the first no-hitter. Boston owner Nathaniel Apollonio rewarded Borden with a three-year contract (multiyear contracts were unheard of at the time) at the then exorbitant salary of $2,000 per year. When Borden failed to live up to expectations, he was made the grounds-keeper to help earn his salary. Dissatisfied with his work as a groundskeeper, Boston bought out his salary. Josephus the Phenomenal was out of baseball at age twenty-two.

2. BUMPUS JONES

On October 14, 1892, the final day of the season, twenty-two-year-old Xenia, Ohio, farmboy Bum-pus Jones walked into the Cincinnati Reds club-house and told manager Charles Comiskey that he wanted to be a big league pitcher. Comiskey decided to give the brash youngster a chance. Bumpus shocked everyone by pitching a no-hitter against the Pittsburgh Pirates in his very first game. He played the game without a contract, making him the greatest bargain in baseball history. Unfortunately, Jones could never recreate the magic of his debut and won only one more game in the majors.

3. EDDIE KOLB

The 1899 Cleveland Spiders were, perhaps, the worst team in baseball history. Managed by an

Australian undertaker named Joe Quinn, the Spiders won only 20 games and lost 134. The team was so bad that Cleveland didn't even want them, and they were forced to play their last 35 games on the road. Not surprisingly, they lost 40 of their last 41 games. On the final day of the season, a clerk at a tobacco shop named Eddie Kolb was permitted to pitch the game in exchange for a box of cigars. True to form, the Spiders lost 19–3.

4. CHARLIE KERFELD

Houston Astros' reliever Charlie Kerfeld was very proud of his uniform number 37. When he signed his contract for the 1987 season, he insisted that he be paid $110,037.37 plus thirty-seven boxes of Jell-O. Weight problems forced the hefty hurler out of baseball at age twenty-three.

5. RUBE WADDELL

Catcher Ossee Schreckengost of the Philadelphia A's was upset when zany pitcher Rube Waddell became his roommate. Waddell had the annoying habit of eating in bed. His midnight snacks included limburger cheese sandwiches and animal crackers. They shared a double bed on the road, and Schreckengost refused to sign his 1903 contract unless the team ordered Waddell to stop eating animal crackers in bed. Schreckengost complained that the crumbs kept him awake.

6. BABE RUTH

Babe Ruth hit 45 home runs and batted in 154 runs in 1929. The next year Yankees' owner Jacob Ruppert offered The Babe a contract for $80,000, the highest in baseball history. When informed by reporters that he was being paid $5,000 more than President Herbert Hoover (who had the misfortune of being president when the stock market crashed), he replied, "I had a better year than he did."

7. THE CINCINNATI RED STOCKINGS

The 1869 Cincinnati Red Stockings were baseball's first all-professional team. The salaries ranged from $600 to $1,400 for star shortstop George Wright. The team toured the country, agreeing to play any team willing to pay them a third of the gate receipts. Over a two-year period, the Red Stockings won a record 130 games without a defeat. They won games by scores of 100–2 and 94–7. Despite the winning streak and minuscule salaries, the club showed a profit of only $1.39.

The 1869 Cincinnati Red Stockings

Despite a record 130-game undefeated streak, baseball's first all professional team, the 1869 Cincinnati Red Stockings, showed only a $1.39 profit.

8. HUGH DUFFY

In 1894, Boston outfielder Hugh Duffy set an all-time major league record when he batted .438. He also led the National League in hits, doubles, home runs, runs batted in, and slugging percentage. The club showed their appreciation by offering Duffy a $12.50 per month raise only if he agreed to become team captain. The captain was responsible for replacing lost equipment. As a result, Duffy actually received a salary cut.

9. KAL DANIELS

Kal Daniels was a hard-hitting outfielder with the Cincinnati Reds in the late 1980s. When contract negotiations stalled in 1989 with the controversial owner Marge Schott, Daniels proposed that they flip a coin to settle the salary dispute. Daniels won the toss and an additional $25,000.

10. JOE PAGE

Joe Page was a star relief pitcher for the championship New York Yankees teams of the late 1940s. Known as much for his late-night carousing, Page was offered one of the first contracts with incentive clauses. His pay varied by as much as $1,000 a month, depending on how well he behaved. Part of the reason for management's concern was that they were afraid Page would corrupt his roommate, superstar outfielder Joe DiMaggio.

Memorable
Memorabilia

Not so many years ago, children collected baseball cards because they wanted to have their own reminders of their favorite players. Packs of cards cost a nickel and came with a rectangular pink stick that, if slowly moistened in your mouth, had a vague resemblance to chewing gum. You would tear through your pack hoping to find a Mickey Mantle or Ted Williams, but you mostly got Whammy Douglas or Rocky Bridges.

Today, baseball card packs often cost several dollars (even without gum). Star players like Ken Griffey Jr. or Roger Clemens are immediately placed in sheets to protect their value. Nobody would think of flipping cards or placing them in the spokes of a bicycle wheel. Baseball collectibles are big business as demonstrated by these examples of memorable memorabilia.

1. HONUS WAGNER

The Holy Grail of baseball collectibles is the Honus Wagner T-206 card. The cards were issued by cigarette companies between 1909 and 1911. Because Wagner objected to smoking, his card was soon withdrawn from circulation. As a result, only a few of the Wagner cards still exist. Hockey great Wayne Gretzky paid $451,000 for one, and it was later sold for more than $600,000.

2. EDDIE MURRAY

In 1996, Eddie Murray of the Baltimore Orioles hit his five hundredth career home run. Collectors were astonished when the fan who retrieved the ball was offered $500,000 for it by the owner of the Psychic Friends Network. The ball's value had been estimated to be no more than $5,000.

3. LOU GEHRIG

A partnership led by David Bowen considered themselves the luckiest men on the face of the earth in the 1990s when they paid $306,130 for the uniform worn by Lou Gehrig in his farewell to baseball on July 4, 1939.

Lou Gehrig

More than 50 years after he retired from baseball,
Lou Gehrig's uniform sold for a record $306,130.

4. PETE ROSE

On September 11, 1985, Pete Rose collected hit
number 4,192 to pass Ty Cobb and become
baseball's all-time hit leader. Rose wore nine different uniforms during the game and sold every
one of them. He also sold the bat that he used to
tie the record for $129,000.

5. BILL BUCKNER

Boston Red Sox's first baseman Bill Buckner became a goat when he let a ground ball go through his legs during the sixth game of the 1986 World Series against the New York Mets. The ball was later purchased by actor Charlie Sheen at an auction for $93,000.

6. DAVID WELLS

New York pitcher David Wells purchased a cap worn by Babe Ruth for $35,000. On June 28, 1997, he wore the hat during the first inning of a game versus the Cleveland Indians. Wells pitched a shutout inning before putting on his own hat. After removing Ruth's cap, Wells was shelled for five runs in two innings.

7. SHOELESS JOE JACKSON

Shoeless Joe Jackson, a .356 lifetime hitter, was banned from baseball because of his involvement in the 1919 Black Sox scandal. In 1990, his signature was sold for $23,100, a record for a nineteenth- or twentieth-century autograph. Jackson was illiterate and copied the signature from one made by his wife.

8. DOUG RADER

Doug Rader played eleven years in the major leagues and managed the Rangers, White Sox, and Angels. Rader sometimes ate baseball cards during the game, saying he believed that he could absorb the statistical information of the opposing players.

9. ERNIE CAMACHO

Pitcher Ernie Camacho complained of a sore arm after an autograph session where he signed 100 photographs. It's hard to imagine that Camacho's signature was that much in demand, considering that he retired in 1988 with a lifetime record of seven wins and twenty losses.

10. GUS ZERNIAL

Everyone has his own favorite unusual baseball card. Some people like the Aurelio Rodriguez card that actually featured a photo of the team's batboy. Others appreciate the card in which Billy Martin extends his middle finger. My favorite is the 1952 Topps card of Philadelphia A's slugging outfielder Gus Zernial. Gus, wearing a pink undershirt and giving the high sign, holds a bat that has five baseballs stuck to it. The significance of the pose remains a mystery.

The naturals

Over the years Hollywood has made many classic baseball movies, from *The Pride of the Yankees* to *The Natural*. Each of the following men had links with both baseball and the movie industry.

1. CHUCK CONNORS

Chuck Connors is best remembered for his role as Lucas McCain in the long-running television series, *The Rifleman*. Connors also starred in *Arrest and Trial*, *Branded*, *Cowboy in Africa*, and the immensely successful miniseries, Roots. Before turning to acting, Connors played professional basketball with the Boston Celtics (once shattering a backboard with a dunk) and from 1949 to 1951 played first base for the Brooklyn Dodgers and Chicago Cubs. He was discovered while playing minor league baseball in Hollywood

Joe DiMaggio
Joe DiMaggio's marriage to actress Marilyn
Monroe lasted only nine months.

and given a small role in the film *Pat and Mike*
starring Spencer Tracy and Katherine Hepburn.

2. JOHN BERARDINO

John Berardino was an infielder in the major
leagues for eleven seasons. During his best season he batted in eighty-nine runs for the 1941 St.
Louis Browns. After his career in baseball was

over, Berardino began a successful acting career. Soap opera devotees will remember him as Dr. Steve Hardy on the popular *General Hospital*.

3. JOE DIMAGGIO

Many consider Joe DiMaggio the greatest all-around player in baseball history. The outfielder starred with the New York Yankees from 1936 to 1951. He married sex symbol Marilyn Monroe in 1954. Although the marriage lasted only nine months, DiMaggio and Monroe remained close until her death in 1962. Shortly after their wedding, Monroe entertained troops stationed in Korea. Marilyn was overwhelmed by the adulation she had received from the soldiers. "You can't imagine what it's like," she told Joe. "Yes, I can," he replied.

4. GENE AUTRY

Gene Autry, Hollywood's "Singing Cowboy," appeared in ninety-three films. An astute businessman, he became a multimillionaire. In 1960, he acquired the expansion California Angels and owned the ballclub for four decades.

5. BOB HOPE

For years, comedian Bob Hope was a minority owner of the Cleveland Indians. Hope had grown up in Cleveland. In 1968, he headed a syndicate prepared to buy the Washington Senators. The deal, however, fell through when Hope became ill.

6. BOB UECKER

Bob Uecker was a major league catcher from 1962 to 1967 with the Cardinals, Braves, and Phillies. A lifetime .200 hitter, he claimed that his biggest thrill was walking with the bases loaded. His self-deprecating humor landed him appearances on *The Tonight Show.* He also starred in the television series, *Mr. Belvedere,* and the film, *Major League.*

7. BEANS REARDON

John "Beans" Reardon was a major league umpire from 1926 to 1949. A friend of actress Mae West, he appeared in five of her films. Reardon got his nickname because of his problem with flatulence. Behind the plate he would often signal a strike by farting and belched when the pitch was a ball. The gas attacks were too much for some catchers, who had to call time out to catch their breath.

8. TURKEY MIKE DONLIN

Outfielder Mike Donlin was perhaps the most popular player of his day and retired in 1914 with a .333 career batting average. He missed several

Jim Bouton

Twenty game winner Jim Bouton wrote a best-selling
tell-all baseball book, *Ball Four,* and appeared in a
film directed by Robert Altman.

seasons in order to tour the vaudeville circuit with
his wife, actress Mabel Hite. He earned the nickname "Turkey Mike" because of his arrogant
strut. Donlin spent the last two decades of his life
producing silent films in Hollywood.

9. BILL MURRAY

When Chicago Cubs' announcer Harry Caray suffered a stroke in the late 1980s, celebrity guest announcers filled in while he recuperated. One of the most memorable was comedian Bill Murray, a lifelong Cub fan. Murray brought his considerable comic skills to the booth. During Wrigley Field's first night game, the opposing leadoff batter hit a home run. Murray suggested that maybe the Cubs should return to all day games.

10. JIM BOUTON

Jim Bouton was a twenty-one-game winner with the New York Yankees in 1963. Seven years later, he authored the best-seller, *Ball Four,* the first tell-all book about baseball. In 1973, Bouton played a leading role in the Robert Altman detective film, *The Long Goodbye.*

Running for Office

Baseball and politics have been linked since April 14, 1910, when President William Howard Taft began a tradition by throwing out the first ball on opening day in Washington. That occasion was marred when Vice President James Sherman was knocked unconscious by a foul ball off the bat of Home Run Baker. Richard Nixon served as an arbiter during a 1985 salary dispute between umpires and management (he granted them a 40 percent salary increase). Each of these men had ties with both baseball and politics.

1. RONALD REAGAN

Ronald Reagan was a radio announcer for the Chicago Cubs before turning to acting. He was discovered in Los Angeles in 1937 when he accompanied the team west for spring training. Reagan got his big break in films when he replaced Ross Alexander, an actor who resembled him, who committed suicide. Reagan was a popular actor before turning to politics. He gained even greater fame when he became governor of California and in 1980 was elected president of the United States.

2. JIM BUNNING

Jim Bunning pitched a perfect game in 1964 and was elected to the Baseball Hall of Fame in 1996. After an unsuccessful campaign for governor of Kentucky in 1984, Bunning was elected to Congress in Kentucky's Fourth District. In 1998 he was elected to the United States Senate.

3. MORGAN BULKELEY

Morgan Bulkeley was the first president of the National League in 1876. After serving four terms as mayor of Hartford, Bulkeley was elected governor of Connecticut. In 1904 he was elected to the United States Senate.

4. JOHN TENER

Tener was a former major league pitcher (1885–90) who served a term in Congress representing Pennsylvania from 1909 to 1911. In 1912, he was elected governor of Pennsylvania, and the following year Tener was named president of the National League. For two years he served in both capacities.

5. FRED BROWN

Fred Brown saw limited action as an outfielder with Boston at the turn of the century. In 1923, Brown was elected governor of New Hampshire and a decade later served a term in the United States Senate.

6. WILMER "VINEGAR BEND" MIZELL

Vinegar Bend Mizell won ninety games in a baseball career that spanned a decade. He was born in Leakesville, Mississippi, but assumed the nickname of a nearby town, Vinegar Bend. (A wise choice, since "Leakesville" Mizell doesn't have the same ring). In 1962, Mizell gave up throwing baseballs to toss his hat into the political ring. He served six terms as a congressman representing a district in North Carolina.

7. DWIGHT EISENHOWER

Dwight Eisenhower was a star halfback at Army (West Point) and a promising baseball player. He batted .355 for Junction City of the Class D Central Kansas League before pursuing a military career. Eisenhower rose to be commander of the Allied forces in Europe during World War II and, in 1952, was elected president of the United States.

8. FIDEL CASTRO

Fidel Castro was a talented pitcher in Cuba with dreams of playing in the major leagues. He was so promising that he was given a tryout by the Washington Senators. Castro was not signed because of his lack of control. Instead of pitching for Washington, Castro became a revolutionary and overthrew the government of Cuba.

9. MARIO CUOMO

In 1951, Mario Cuomo was given a $2,000 bonus by the Pittsburgh Pirates. The next year the young outfielder was hitting over .350 when he injured his wrist crashing into a wall. Hot tempered, Mario once punched a catcher after he had made an ethnic slur. Unfortunately, the catcher was still wearing his mask, and Cuomo bruised his fingers. His promising career abruptly ended when he was beaned. Cuomo suffered a blood clot and was hospitalized for weeks. Doctors warned him that a similar beaning might be fatal. With his major league aspirations crushed, Cuomo embarked on a political career that culminated with his election as governor of New York.

10. HAPPY CHANDLER

A. B. "Happy" Chandler served two terms as governor of Kentucky and six years in the United

States Senate. His term as commissioner of base-ball from 1945 to 1951 was noteworthy because of the elimination of the color barrier.

Out of Their League

Many professional baseball players have excelled in other sports. For example, Earle "Greasy" Neale played eight seasons as an outfielder with the Cincinnati Reds and later coached the Philadelphia Eagles to NFL championships in 1948 and 1949. In 1960, Pittsburgh shortstop Dick Groat was the National League Most Valuable Player. Before he played professional baseball, Groat was a two-time All-American basketball player at Duke and played a season with the Fort Wayne Pistons in the NBA. Here are some of the most accomplished two sport stars.

1. JIM THORPE

Jim Thorpe has often been called the world's greatest all-around athlete. He was the first athlete to win the gold medal in the decathlon, a feat that he accomplished at the 1912 Olympics.

Thorpe was forced to return the medal when it was learned he had briefly played professional baseball in the minor leagues in 1909. He played six years in the majors, hitting .327 in 1919. Thorpe had greater success in the NFL and was elected to the Pro Football Hall of Fame in 1963.

2. GEORGE HALAS

George Halas played in twelve games for the New York Yankees in 1919, batting an anemic .091. Halas was one of the founders of the National Football League and played eleven seasons on both defense and offense. He coached the Chicago Bears to six NFL championships, and his 325 wins set a record, which stood until 1993 when it was broken by Don Shula.

3. ERNIE NEVERS

Ernie Nevers's baseball career was undistinguished (a 6–12 record with the St. Louis Browns). On the gridiron, his play earned him induction into both the College and Pro Football Halls of Fame. His coach at Stanford, the legendary "Pop" Warner, called him "the greatest player I ever coached." Nevers set an NFL record when he scored forty points in a game against the Chicago Bears in 1929.

4. BO JACKSON

A commercial campaign by Nike suggested Bo Jackson knew how to play any sport. In football, the running back was good enough to win the Heisman Trophy. He announced that he intended to play both professional baseball and football, labeling his NFL career a "hobby." In 1989, he slugged 32 home runs and batted in 105 runs for the Kansas City Royals. His two-sport stardom ended when he suffered a devastating hip injury while playing for the Raiders. After hip replacement surgery, Jackson's football career was over, and his baseball skills declined.

5. DEION SANDERS

Deion Sanders was selected as one of the greatest cornerbacks on the 75th NFL anniversary team. "Neon Deion" played on Super Bowl champions in both San Francisco and Dallas. On the diamond, Sanders played outfield for the Yankees, Giants, and Reds. He played well enough to hit over .300 one season and was usually among the league leaders in stolen bases.

6. DAVE DEBUSSCHERE

Dave DeBusschere was a good enough pitcher with the Chicago White Sox to post a career 2.90

earned run average in his two seasons in the majors in 1962 and 1963. He gave up baseball to play professional basketball full time. During his twelve-season NBA career, DeBusschere scored over 14,000 points and played on championship teams with the New York Knicks. Other notable athletes who played in both major league baseball and the NBA include Ron Reed, Danny Ainge, and Gene Conley.

7. JACKIE JENSEN

Jackie Jensen was an All-American fullback at the University of California. A thousand-yard rusher, he ran sixty-seven yards for a touchdown in the Rose Bowl. He chose to play major league baseball instead of pro football. Brought up by the New York Yankees in 1950, he was groomed to be the replacement for Joe DiMaggio. Beaten out of the starting center field job by Mickey Mantle, Jensen later starred for the Boston Red Sox. He led the American League in runs batted in for three years and was the stolen base champion in 1954. He retired in 1961 at the peak of his career, partly due to an extreme fear of flying.

8. BILL SHARMAN

Bill Sharman teamed in the backcourt with Bob Cousy on several Boston Celtics' championship

Jackie Jensen

Before he became an All-Star outfielder for the
Boston Red Sox, Jackie Jensen was an All-American running back for the University of California.

teams. One of the greatest free throw shooters in
NBA history (88.3 percent), he was elected to the
Pro Basketball Hall of Fame in 1975. He had one
of the shortest and strangest careers in the major
leagues. Called up to the major leagues by Brooklyn in late 1951, Sharman rode the bench as the
Dodgers blew a huge lead in the final month. On
September 27, umpire Frank Dascoli threw out
every player in the Brooklyn dugout, including

Sharman. As a result, he became the only player in major league history to be thrown out of a game while never playing in one.

9. RANDY "MACHO MAN" SAVAGE

Randy Poffo was a minor league catcher in the Cardinals' and Reds' farm systems during the early 1970s. When he failed to reach the major leagues, he turned to professional wrestling. His father, Angelo Poffo, had been the United States wrestling champion. Billing himself as "Macho Man" Savage, Randy eventually won both the World Wrestling Federation and World Championship Wrestling titles.

10. MICHAEL JORDAN

Widely considered to be the greatest player in NBA history, Michael Jordan had led the Chicago Bulls to three championships when he decided to try professional baseball. With a batting average hovering around the .200 mark in the minors, Jordan never made it to the major leagues. Returning to basketball, he led the Bulls to three more NBA titles.

Playing the Field

Since major league baseball players spend so much time on the road, it's not surprising that some of them carry on highly active sex lives. Former Angels' general manager Dick "The Smiling Python" Walsh once threatened to tell a pitcher's wife about an adulterous affair if he didn't sign the contract offered. When Manager Leo Durocher was suspended from baseball for a year, one of the reasons was adultery. This section includes a rogues' gallery of baseball Casanovas.

1. BO BELINSKY

Baseball's undisputed Don Juan, Belinsky had a mediocre career as a pitcher (28–51 lifetime record), highlighted by a no-hitter against Baltimore in 1962. Off the field, he fashioned a Hall of Fame love life. Among the women Bo dated were Ann-Margret, Tina Louise, Connie Stevens,

Juliet Prowse, and the Shah of Iran's ex-wife, Queen Soraya. His most publicized romance was to blonde bombshell Mamie Van Doren. When they broke up, Bo lamented, "I needed her like Custer needed more Indians." Belinsky eventually married 1965 Playmate of the Year, Jo Collins.

Angels' publicity director Irv Kaze described Belinsky's appeal, "He's a handsome son of a bitch. You can almost feel the animal sex in him." Teammates recalled Belinsky stepping off a plane into the arms of three waiting women. On another occasion, Belinsky discovered a young lady hanging by her fingertips on the window sill outside his hotel room. "I had no choice but to let her in," Bo quipped. He claimed sex helped him relax. "No one ever died of it," Bo observed.

2. BABE RUTH

Babe Ruth was a man of large appetites. This carried over into his sex life. Author Fred Lieb noted, "One woman couldn't satisfy him. Frequently it took half a dozen." Ruth preferred the company of prostitutes and bragged that he had once had sex with every woman at a St. Louis brothel. Because the media in those days did not focus on the private lives of ballplayers, most of Ruth's fans were unaware of his sexual exploits.

3. **JOE PEPITONE**

Although Joe Pepitone hit 219 home runs, he never achieved the stardom that was expected of him. His downfall was a less than exemplary personal life. Pepitone was especially vain about his appearance, endlessly combing his hair. He was the first player to bring a hair dryer into the clubhouse and wore flashy clothes. Diane, his second wife, was said to have found slips of paper with the names of 150 women with whom Joe had sex. In 1974, Pepitone married a former Playboy bunny.

Joe Pepitone
Power-hitting first baseman Joe Pepitone was also a hit with the ladies.

4. STEVE GARVEY

For nineteen years, Steve Garvey was a star first baseman for the Los Angeles Dodgers and San Diego Padres. Six times he collected more than 200 hits and played in 1,207 consecutive games. For most of his career, he had an image of being baseball's "Mr. Clean." The clean-cut facade was shattered after a nasty divorce from his college sweetheart, Cyndi, in 1985. His sex life made headlines when it was revealed that he had impregnated two women just as he was about to marry a third.

5. PETE ROSE

Baseball's all-time hit leader, Pete Rose, had the reputation of being a womanizer. It was rumored that Rose had a mistress in each National League city. After his divorce from first wife Karolyn in 1984, he married Carol Woliung, a stunning blonde Playboy bunny and Philadelphia Eagles cheerleader. Rose joked that he got all the women because he always went in head first.

6. WADE BOGGS

The winner of five American League batting titles, Wade Boggs was considered the consummate hitter. In 1988, a story broke that the All-Star third baseman had been having an affair with an investment broker named Margo Adams. For four years, the two had traveled together on road trips while Boggs's wife, Debbie, remained home, unaware of the affair. Adams learned that Boggs was seeing other women and got revenge by having an affair with Steve Garvey. When Boggs attempted to end the relationship, Adams demanded $100,000 or she would reveal the affair to his wife. Boggs refused, and Margo filed a $11.5 million breach-of-contract suit, claiming she had performed various duties ranging from providing financial advice to washing his clothes. Adams received $100,000 for baring all in *Penthouse Magazine*. Boggs returned to his wife, stating that the revelations had made his marriage stronger.

7. VAN LINGLE MUNGO

The man with the lyrical name and the blazing fastball, Van Lingle Mungo was a somnambulist. When he wasn't walking in his sleep, he was sleeping with women. His most famous escapade occurred in Cuba where the Dodgers were training in 1941. According to Leo Durocher, Mungo was caught in bed with two women by one of their husbands. The Dodgers arranged to smuggle the pitcher out of the country. With the machete-wielding cuckold in close pursuit, Mungo was pulled inside an awaiting plane just in the nick of time, an escape worthy of Indiana Jones.

8. TILLIE SHAFER

Tillie Shafer was an infielder for the New York Giants between 1909 and 1913. He was known as the "Perfumed Note Man" because of the scented invitations he received from his many lady admirers.

9. FRITZ PETERSON AND MIKE KEKICH

New York Yankees' pitchers Fritz Peterson and Mike Kekich pulled off baseball's strangest trade in 1972. Peterson and Kekich swapped wives, children, pets, and even their station wagons. "It wasn't a wife swap; it was a life swap," Kekich concluded.

10. LOU SOCKALEXIS

John McGraw said that Lou Sockalexis was the greatest talent he had ever seen in baseball. The outfielder, a Penobscot Indian, destroyed a potentially great career through his excesses off the field. He was batting .338 during his rookie season in 1897 when he injured his foot jumping from the window of a whorehouse while celebrating the Fourth of July. Another time, he was so disoriented by a sexual marathon that he was barely able to stagger out on the field. He played in only ninety-four games, a career ruined by alcohol and women.

The Fair Sex

Although a woman has never played in a major league game, several women have had an impact on the game.

1. HELENE BRITTON

Long before Marge Schott was even born, Helene Britton became the first woman to own a major league team. She presided over the St. Louis Cardinals from 1911 to 1917. Although she met resistance from most of the male owners, she proved to be a capable executive and oversaw the day-to-day operations of the club.

2. JACKIE MITCHELL

Jackie Mitchell was the first woman to sign a professional baseball contract. In 1931, the left-handed pitcher signed to play for the minor league Chattanooga Lookouts. On April 2, 1931,

Mitchell pitched in an exhibition game against the mighty New York Yankees. The seventeen-year-old stunned the crowd by striking out Babe Ruth and Lou Gehrig. The next day Baseball Commissioner Kenesaw Mountain Landis barred women from playing professional baseball. His excuse was that baseball was "too strenuous for a woman to play."

3. BABE DIDRIKSON

Babe Didrikson is often called the greatest woman athlete of all time. She won two gold medals at the 1932 Summer Olympics and later became a champion golfer, winning thirty-one tournaments. In 1934, she pitched several games in spring training against major league opposition. Pitching for the Philadelphia A's, Didrikson pitched a shutout inning against Brooklyn.

4. ILA BORDERS

On May 31, 1997, Ila Borders became the first woman to play in a minor league game. Borders pitched for the St. Paul Saints against Sioux Falls. She gave up three runs without retiring a batter. The next day, Borders redeemed herself by striking out the side in a second relief appearance.

5. **KITTY BURKE**

Kitty Burke holds the distinction of being the only woman to come to the plate during a major league game. On July 31, 1935, Burke was one of the more than 30,000 spectators at Cincinnati's Crosley Field watching the Reds play the St. Louis Cardinals. The sellout crowd was so large that thousands of the spectators were permitted to stand on the field in foul territory. In the eighth inning, Babe Herman of the Reds stepped to the plate. Burke, who had been heckling batters all night, walked up and grabbed the bat from Herman. To everyone's amazement, pitcher Paul "Daffy" Dean threw her a pitch, which she grounded to an infielder. Frankie Frisch, the Cardinals' manager, argued that it should be the third out. The umpire disagreed, and Herman doubled as the Reds rallied for a 4–3 victory.

6. **JOAN PAYSON**

Joan Payson owned the New York Mets from 1962 to 1975. Under her ownership, the Mets were transformed from a hapless expansion team to world champions in 1969. Originally, Payson wanted to name the team the New York Meadowlarks.

7. MRS. CHARLEY JONES

Charley Jones was one of baseball's first sluggers. In 1879, he led the National League in home runs and runs batted in. A handsome grandstand idol, Jones was paid by a Cincinnati clothier for just walking around town wearing the tailor's latest styles. On one of these strolls, he was accompanied by another woman. His wife, not understanding the value of good advertising, threw cayenne pepper in his eyes, effectively ending his career.

8. HELEN DAUVRAY

Helen Dauvray was a popular actress in the late nineteenth century and the wife of New York Giants' shortstop John Montgomery Ward. At the time the National League and American Association, two established major leagues, played a World Series at the end of the season. Dauvray talked the owners into commissioning Tiffany's to design a silver cup that would be given to the first team to win three championship series. The Dauvray Cup was retired in 1891 when the American Association folded.

9. BEATRICE GERA

For years Beatrice Gera fought in court to have the opportunity to become the first woman professional umpire. Finally, on June 25, 1972, Gera was given her chance in a minor league game in Geneva, New York. When Auburn manager Nolan Campbell argued a close call, Gera burst into tears and resigned after one game. However, her efforts did clear the way for successful lady umps, such as Pam Postema, who umpired in the minor leagues for thirteen years.

10. MORGANNA, THE KISSING BANDIT

Morganna Roberts is an exotic dancer whose most noticeable asset is her sixty-inch bust. She has left her mark on the national pastime by running on the field and kissing players. Morganna has planted kisses on more than twenty-five players, including Pete Rose, Nolan Ryan, and Mike Schmidt. George Brett found the experience disconcerting. "After looking at her chest," he remembered, "it made the ball look like a pencil dot."

Clothes Encounters

On June 19, 1846, the first recorded baseball game was played between the New York Nine and the New York Knickerbockers. The Knickerbockers wore the first uniforms: blue trousers, white shirts, and straw hats. While players are required to wear their teams' uniforms, occasionally someone will come up with his own variation. Cleveland pitcher Johnny Allen wore a tattered sleeve on his uniform to distract batters. Big Ted Kluszewski, while playing for the Cincinnati Reds in the 1950s, wore no sleeves on his uniform to show off his massive arms. Here are some players whose uniforms were anything but uniform. As Yogi Berra once said, "I have every color of sweater except navy brown."

1. BOBBY BRAGAN

Bobby Bragan managed the Pirates, Indians, and Braves between 1956 and 1966. Bragan was notorious for his disputes with umpires. He was catching for the minor league Hollywood Stars when he argued a call at home plate. In disgust, he removed his chest protector, shin guards, mask, and cap. He continued the striptease in the dugout, throwing his uniform, shoes, and undershirt onto the field.

2. **GERMANY SCHAEFER**

Second baseman Germany Schaefer played in the major leagues from 1901 until 1918. Schaefer is best remembered for his outrageous antics on the field. During one rainy game he came to the plate wearing a raincoat and boots.

3. **DAN FRIEND**

On August 30, 1897, the Chicago Cubs were playing the New York Giants. The game was in the ninth inning, and the Cub pitcher had already showered when he was ordered to go in and play left field to replace a player who had been ejected. Friend trotted to his position wearing a bathrobe and his baseball cap.

4. **WILLIE WELLS**

Willie "the Devil" Wells was one of the best shortstops in the Negro League. In 1926, he suffered a serious beaning. The next time he came to bat, Wells was wearing a miner's hat to protect his head. The pitcher drilled him in the side, injuring his ribs.

5. JOHN COLEMAN

Philadelphia pitcher John Coleman was unexpectedly called in to replace an injured rightfielder in the sixth inning of a game on May 10, 1885. Coleman was so unprepared that he played the rest of the game in street clothes.

6. CONNIE MACK

Connie Mack managed the Philadelphia A's for fifty years. Rather than wear a uniform, Mack sat on the bench dressed in a suit and tie. During the 1890s, Baltimore manager Ned Hanlon frequently wore a silk top hat and spats.

7. THE 1882 NATIONAL LEAGUE UNIFORMS

In 1882, the National League experimented with color-coded uniforms. Each position had a different color uniform: first base (scarlet and white), second base (orange and black), shortstop (maroon), third base (gray and white), right field (gray), center field (red and black), left field (white), catcher (scarlet), and pitcher (blue). Since the uniforms did not yet have numbers, it was hoped that the color-coded uniforms would make it easier for the fans to identify the players. The experiment proved unpopular and was soon dropped.

8. **FRANK LACORTE**

On May 26, 1982, Houston pitcher Frank LaCorte walked the bases loaded in a game against the Montreal Expos. He was so angry with his performance that he burned his uniform in the clubhouse.

9. **FRANK COGGINS**

Frank Coggins was a utility player with the Washington Senators in the late 1960s. Coggins is remembered as one of the flashiest dressers in baseball history. A typical outfit would be a pink suit, knickers, and a straw hat. After his playing days were over, Coggins was employed by the FBI.

10. **THE 1976 CHICAGO WHITE SOX UNIFORMS**

One of owner Bill Veeck's least appreciated innovations was the uniform he unveiled for the 1976 Chicago White Sox. The players were forced to wear shorts—and endure the snickers of fans and opposing players.

Smarter than the Average Berra

On the whole, baseball players are not known for their intellectual endeavors. When asked if he knew of any literate players, the author W. P. Kinsella replied, "Tom Seaver is the only one who comes to mind. I do know that Steve Boros reads." Actually, some players have exhibited brain as well as brawn.

1. MOE BERG

Catcher Moe Berg was undoubtedly one of the most intelligent players to ever play professional baseball. A magna cum laude graduate of Princeton, he received a law degree from Columbia and studied philosophy at the Sorbonne in Paris. He declined an offer to teach in the romance language department at Princeton in order to play professional baseball.

John Montgomery Ward
Hall of Famer John Montgomery Ward was a
successful attorney, author, agent, and labor
leader.

Unfortunately, his baseball skills did not com-
pare with his mental gifts. Brooklyn scout Mike
Gonzalez coined the phrase, "good field, no hit"
after watching Berg play. Pitcher Ted Lyons
joked, "He can speak ten languages and can't hit
in any of them." In fifteen seasons, Berg hit only
six home runs. As a backup catcher, he spent
most of his time in the bullpen. Each morning he

bought at least a dozen foreign newspapers, which he would read during the game. He was the only player who kept a tuxedo hung in his locker.

As World War II approached, Berg used his linguistic abilities to serve his country. During a tour of American All-Stars in Japan before the war, Berg took espionage photos of Tokyo. After the war started, Berg posed as a Swiss businessman and German officer in order to attempt to obtain German atomic secrets.

Years later, Berg was offered a $35,000 advance to write an autobiography. He declined the offer when his editor mistook him for Moe Howard of the Three Stooges.

2. JOHN MONTGOMERY WARD

John Montgomery Ward was one of the most remarkable figures in baseball history. As a nineteen-year-old pitcher, he won forty-seven games, and the next season pitched a perfect game. His 2.10 career earned run average is the fourth lowest in baseball history. When he injured his pitching arm, Ward became a shortstop and collected over 2,000 hits. He was elected to the Baseball Hall of Fame in 1964.

Ward attended Penn State University and received his law degree from Columbia. He founded the first players' union, the Brotherhood, in 1885.

Five years later, he led the players to form their own league that competed with the established National League for a year. Ward wrote articles in the leading publications of the day on subjects ranging from psychology to human rights. He became a successful attorney, was the first player's agent, and was nearly elected president of the National League.

3. TED LEWIS

A twenty-game winner with Boston in 1897 and 1898, Ted Lewis retired at age twenty-nine to coach baseball at Harvard. He later taught English at Columbia University and was president of Massachusetts State College. The final nine years of his life, Lewis served as president of the University of New Hampshire. He sometimes discussed poetry and played catch in his backyard with the poet Robert Frost.

4. JAY HOOK

One of the original New York Mets, Jay Hook had a miserable 29–62 career record. He pitched the Mets to their first victory and was responsible for giving first baseman Marv Throneberry his nickname, "Marvelous." Hook earned a master's degree in mechanical engineering from Northwestern University. He wrote an article in the *New*

York Times explaining why a breaking ball curved. Apparently, the batters in the National League must have read the article before they faced Hook. A loser on the field, Hook became a big winner in the business world. He became a vice president at MASCO, a Detroit conglomerate, where he was in charge of making multimillion dollar deals.

5. DAVE BALDWIN

Dave Baldwin was a solid reliever who had a terrific 1.70 earned run average as a rookie with Washington in 1967. During his playing days Baldwin was an anthropologist in the off-season. In 1979, he earned a Ph.D. in genetics and four years later received his M.S. in systems engineering. Baldwin also published numerous scientific articles, children's stories, and humor pieces.

6. GEORGE DAVIS

On September 9, 1914, George Davis, a Harvard law student, pitched a no-hitter for the Boston Braves against Philadelphia. The next season the promising young pitcher retired to practice law.

7. JIM BROSNAN

Reliever Jim Brosnan was nicknamed "The Professor" because of his scholarly demeanor. Brosnan helped lead Cincinnati to the pennant in

1961, finishing with a 10–4 record. His journal of the pennant race, *The Long Season,* became a baseball classic. He wrote a second book, *Pennant Race,* as well as articles for *Sports Illustrated* and other publications. His writing was not appreciated by the baseball establishment because of its honest depiction of what took place behind clubhouse doors, and the Chicago White Sox sent Brosnan a contract in 1964 that forbade him to publish. Brosnan placed an ad in *The Sporting News* that read, "Free agent. Negotiable terms available. Respectfully request permission to pursue harmless avocation of professional writer." Forced to choose between baseball and writing, Brosnan chose the pen over the bullpen.

8. **BOBBY BROWN**

Bobby Brown was a third baseman for the New York Yankees from 1946 to 1954. His greatest moments came in four World Series in which he hit a combined .439. Brown attended Stanford, UCLA, and Tulane University School of Medicine. After retiring from baseball, he practiced cardiology in Fort Worth, Texas. From 1984 to 1994 he served as American League president.

9. **BEN OGLIVIE**

Ben Oglivie was a power-hitting outfielder from Panama who led the American League in home

Bobby Brown
Bobby Brown played in
four World Series with
the Yankees and later
became a successful
cardiologist and President
of the American League.

runs (41) in 1980. Oglivie was more than just a
smart hitter. He had wide intellectual interests and
could finish a *New York Times* crossword puzzle
in fifteen minutes. Teammates would find him
engrossed in reading Jean-Jacques Rousseau or
some other brainy material.

10. KEN HOLTZMAN

Lefthander Ken Holtzman won twenty-one games
in 1973 and was one of the aces on the Oakland A's
championship teams. Nicknamed "the Thinker,"
he read Marcel Proust's seven-volume master-
piece, *Remembrance of Things Past* in the original
French.

Stengelese and Other Tongues

B aseball players have a language that is all their own. It makes perfect sense to them, but something is lost in the translation for the rest of us. Here are some of the leading purveyors of baseball speak.

1. YOGI BERRA

Yogi Berra was a Hall of Fame catcher and a pennant-winning manager, but his most lasting contribution to American culture may be his unique use of language. Describing the creeping shadows in left field, Yogi commented, "It gets late early out there." Yogi on the shrinking dollar: "A nickel ain't worth a dime anymore." When the Yankees held a Yogi Berra Night in his honor, Yogi quipped, "Thank you for making this night necessary." Two classic Yogiisms, "It was déjà vu all over again" and "It ain't over till it's over," have become catch phrases (no pun intended).

Casey Stengel
Fired after leading the New York Yankees to
their tenth pennant in twelve years, manager
Casey Stengel remarked, "I'll never make the
mistake of being 70 again."

When Yogi's wife Carmen told him she had
just seen *Dr. Zhivago,* a concerned Yogi asked,
"Oh, what's the matter with you, now?" On watching Steve McQueen in *The Magnificent Seven,*
Berra observed, "He made that movie before he
died." With these remarkable perceptions, it was
only natural that Berra be asked to review films
on television. Yogi referred to the star of *Dirty
Harry* as Cliff Eastwick. While reviewing Neil

Simon's *Biloxi Blues,* he informed viewers, "It reminded me of being in the army, even though I was in the navy." Berra denied that he was responsible for all the quotes attributed to him, "I didn't say everything I said."

2. CASEY STENGEL

Casey Stengel managed the New York Yankees to ten pennants between 1947 and 1960. The "Old Perfesser" once told his players, "Now all you fellers line up alphabetically by height." In July 1958, Stengel appeared before the U. S. Senate subcommittee antitrust hearings and befuddled politicians used to doubletalk with an hour of Stengelese. When an aging Casey was fired after the 1960 season, despite winning the pennant, he lamented, "I'll never make the mistake of being seventy again." Casey's epitaph says it all: "There comes a time in every man's life, at least once, and I've had plenty of them."

3. JERRY COLEMAN

Jerry Coleman played second base for the New York Yankees from 1949 to 1957. His most memo- rable moments have come as an announcer for the San Diego Padres. Coleman's propensity for the verbal miscue has his listeners hanging on every word. Coleman's "sun-blown pop-ups" and play- ers "sliding into second base with a stand-up double" may confuse the uninitiated but delight the devotees. Who could ever forget Coleman's line, "Rich Folkers is throwing up in the bullpen"? Undoubtedly, Jerry's finest moment came when he described Padres' outfielder Dave Winfield chasing a long fly: "Winfield is going back. He hits his head against the wall. It's rolling back toward second base."

Choo Choo Coleman

One of the original New York Mets, catcher Choo Choo Coleman had such trouble giving signals to the pitcher that it was suggested that he color code his fingers.

4. PHIL RIZZUTO

Phil Rizzuto played shortstop on the Yankee team with Casey Stengel, Yogi Berra, and Jerry Coleman. One can only imagine the conversations this foursome would have during a game of bridge. The Scooter was a better player than his double play partner, Jerry Coleman, and almost his equal as an announcer. Rizzuto's specialties are inattention to detail, occasional lapses of memory, and meaningless anecdotes that he forgets to finish. Rizzuto once expressed amazement that Johnny Neun had managed the Yankees even though he had played while he was manager. Another time, he was worried that star pitcher Ron Guidry might have been struck by a line drive hit into the Yankees dugout. Rizzuto had failed to notice that Guidry was on the mound.

5. CHOO CHOO COLEMAN

Clarence "Choo Choo" Coleman was a catcher with the original New York Mets, perhaps the worst baseball team of the century. Coleman had dubious defensive skills, a .197 career batting average, and a way with words only his manager Casey Stengel could appreciate. Choo Choo had such a problem giving signals to the pitcher that the Mets considered painting his fingers blue for fast ball, red for curve, green for change-up. At the end of the season, teammate Charlie Neal confronted Choo Choo, "I bet you don't know who I am." Coleman replied, "You're number 4." Ralph Kiner asked him his wife's name and what she was like. Choo Choo answered, "Her name is Mrs. Coleman, and she likes me."

6. DIZZY DEAN

Dizzy Dean was the last National League pitcher to win thirty games in a season (1934), and his mangling of the English language as an announcer paved the way for ex-players such as Jerry Coleman to enter the booth. When Dizzy was knocked unconscious during a game, the headlines the next day read: "Dean's Head Examined: X-Rays Reveal Nothing." Dean described players being "purply [purposely] passed," "returning to their respectable bases," and "sludding into third." Dizzy, who admitted to flunking out of the second grade, was assailed by English teachers because of his prolific use of the word "ain't." Diz silenced his critics by saying, "A lot of people who don't say ain't ain't eatin."

7. RALPH KINER

Ralph Kiner led the National League in home runs for seven consecutive years and probably leads National League announcers in messing up players' names. The Mets star catcher, Gary Carter, became "Gary Cooper." Kiner called third baseman Tim Wallach "Eli Wallach" so many times that his teammates nicknamed him Eli. Two of Kiner's most hilarious misnomers were calling Dan Driessen "Diana Driessen" and referring to Don Bilardello as "Don Bordello."

8. DANNY OZARK

Danny Ozark managed the Philadelphia Phillies to three consecutive divisional titles from 1976 to 1978. Ozark earned the reputation as the Master of the Malaprop. After his club had blown a huge lead, Ozark lamented, "Even Napoleon had his Watergate." When his team was mathematically eliminated from the pennant race, an upbeat Ozark vowed, "We're not out of it yet."

9. HARRY CARAY

The voice of the Chicago Cubs for two decades, colorful Harry Caray was a bigger celebrity than most of the team's players. Harry's distinctive play-by-play style included reading the names of most anyone who was attending or watching the game. Fans were well aware of his much-expressed love of alcohol. He once referred to outfielder Dave Collins as Tom Collins. During a promo for Budweiser, he said, "I'm a Gub fan and

a Bud man." Doctors advised Caray to give up
drinking in 1994. They said he could take another
drink when the Cubs won their next pennant. They
won their last in 1945.

10. **MICKEY RIVERS**

Outfielder Mickey Rivers was known as "Mick the
Quick" because of his extraordinary speed.
During his playing days from 1970 to 1984, he
exhibited verbal skills not heard in New York since
the retirement of Yogi Berra. "What is the name of
the dog on *Rin Tin Tin?*" Rivers asked. He stated
that his goals were to "hit .300, score 100 runs,
and stay injury-prone." Comparing the weather in
New York and his native Florida, Rivers remarked,
"The climax is about the same." Asked if he got
along with owner George Steinbrenner and manager Billy Martin, Mickey replied, "Me and George
and Billy, we're two of a kind."

Notable Nicknames

Many baseball players have nicknames. Babe Ruth was the "Sultan of Swat." Ted Williams was known as the "Splendid Splinter." Not every nickname is as well known. Jimmy Bannon's nickname was "Foxy Grandpa." Bris Lord was the "Human Eyeball." Pearce "What's the Use" Chiles's nickname says all you need to know about his career. For some players their nicknames are their main claim to fame: John "Pretzels" Pezzullo, Clarence "Cupid" Childs, Joe "Horse Belly" Sargent, Harry "Stinky" Davis, Walter "Cuckoo" Christenson, and George "White Wings" Tebeau. ESPN's Chris Berman gained notoriety for giving players whimsical nicknames (e.g., Oddibe "Young Again" McDowell). This section features baseball's most intriguing nicknames.

1. DEATH TO FLYING THINGS

Bob Ferguson earned the sobriquet "Death to Flying Things" because of his uncanny ability as a fielder. Baseball's first switch hitter, he scored the winning run for the Brooklyn Atlantics in 1870 to end the Cincinnati Red Stockings' record-winning streak. A no-nonsense competitor, Ferguson later became an umpire and broke a batter's arm with a bat during an argument.

2. THE FRESHEST MAN ON EARTH

Arlie Latham was one of the fastest players of his day. In 1887, while playing for St. Louis, the third baseman stole 129 bases and scored 163 runs. Latham was known as the "Freshest Man on Earth" because of his ebullient personality. After retirement, Latham spent sixteen years in England where he was a personal friend to King George V and taught the monarch the fine points of baseball.

3. TOMATO FACE

Outfielder Nick Cullop was given the nickname "Tomato Face" because his face turned bright red every time he became angry. In 1931, his final season, Cullop was frequently red-faced as he led the National League in striking out.

4. WAGON TONGUE

Bill "Wagon Tongue" Keister had a .312 lifetime batting average. Keister got his nickname because he rarely stopped talking. Unfortunately he was one of the worst fielding shortstops in baseball history. In 1901, he set the all-time record for the lowest single season fielding percentage (.861). Because he was such a liability in the field, "Wagon Tongue" played for a different team in each of his seven seasons.

5. THE NERVOUS GREEK

Lou Skizas got his nickname "The Nervous Greek" because of the strange ritual he performed every time he came to the plate. The outfielder played for the Yankees, A's, Tigers, and White Sox between 1956 and 1959. Before he stepped into the batter's box Skizas walked between the catcher and the umpire, rubbed the bat between his legs, and reached into his back pocket to touch a lucky Greek coin he kept there. He hit .314 as a rookie but his luck soon ran out, and by 1959 his average had nose-dived to .077.

6. THE APOLLO OF THE BOX

Pitcher Tony Mullane was known as the "Apollo of the Box" because of his good looks. The handsome righthander from Cork, Ireland, was so popular with female fans that the Cincinnati Red Stockings initiated Ladies Day every Monday when he pitched. Mullane won thirty games his first five full seasons and had 285 victories during his career, which lasted from 1881 to 1894. He also has the distinction of being the first ambidextrous pitcher.

7. LADY

In 1886, Charles Baldwin set a National League record for lefthanders when he won forty-two games. Baldwin employed an unusual hop-skip-and-jump delivery similar to a cricket player. When the delivery was outlawed the following season, Baldwin's effectiveness declined. He was nicknamed "Lady" by his teammates because he didn't drink, smoke, or curse. Ironically, his middle name was Busted.

8. THE HUMAN RAIN DELAY

Mike Hargrove is best known for managing the Cleveland Indians to their first pennant in forty years. As a player, the first baseman batted over .300 five times during his career from 1974 until 1985. He was known as "The Human Rain Delay" because of his deliberate ritual in the batter's box. The stalling tactic was so unnerving to pitchers that Hargrove twice led the league in walks.

9. **THE MAD MONK**

Russ Meyer won ninety-four games during his thirteen-year major-league career that ended in 1959. Nicknamed the "Mad Monk" because of his temper, he was a notorious bench jockey. After one bad outing, he threw his spikes into the shower, where they stuck in the ceiling.

10. **BLIMP**

In 1936, Babe Phelps set an all-time record for catchers when he batted .367 for the Brooklyn Dodgers. He might have done even better, but he had the bizarre habit of staying awake all night to listen to his heartbeat. Phelps was convinced that if his heart skipped four beats he would die. Babe was given the nickname "Blimp" because of his shape. Despite his nickname, he had an intense fear of flying and retired in 1940 when teams began traveling by air. From that time on he was referred to as the "Grounded Blimp."

Hot Dogs

Fans consume thousands of hot dogs a year while watching baseball games. The term has also been used to describe players with a tendency to show off. Enjoy the following line-up of hot dogs.

1. REGGIE JACKSON

Pitcher Darold Knowles said of Reggie Jackson, "There's not enough mustard in the world to cover that hot dog." Jackson personified "hot dog" during his flamboyant twenty-one-year career. He hit 563 home runs (sixth on the all-time list), but he also struck out a record 2,597 times. Reggie often would stand at home plate to admire his tape-measure home runs. He received the attention he coveted when he was traded to the New York Yankees in 1977. "I didn't come to New York to become a star," he modestly declared. "I brought my own star." Referring to himself as the "straw that stirs the drink," he was considered the "straw that broke the camel's back" by some teammates. When they came out with a candy bar named Reggie in his honor, sportswriter Dave Anderson said, "It's the only candy bar that tastes like a hot dog."

2. MIKE "KING" KELLY

King Kelly was one of the most popular and accomplished players of the nineteenth century. Playing every position during his career, he led his teams to nine pennants. He twice led the National League in hitting and batted .388 in 1886. More than any other player, Kelly enjoyed the spotlight. In his book, *Play Ball,* he wrote, "Every baseball club must have a star, just as a dramatic company must have a leading man." Kelly perfected the "Kelly Spread," an early version of the hook slide. The cry of "slide, Kelly, slide" was heard at ballparks throughout the National League. His most famous exploit occurred while he was managing Boston. An opposing player hit a pop fly near the dugout. The quick-witted manager announced, "Kelly now catching for Boston," and caught the ball for an out.

3. DIZZY DEAN

Jay "Dizzy" Dean was a Hall of Fame pitcher and a world-class hot dog. He constantly bragged about his pitching prowess and was usually able to back up his boasts. Prior to the 1934 season, Dizzy predicted that he and his brother "Daffy" would win at least forty-five games for the Cardinals. The Deans exceeded Dizzy's expectations by winning a combined forty-nine games. In September of that year, Dizzy pitched a three-hit shutout in the first game of a doubleheader versus Brooklyn. After brother "Daffy" no-hit the Dodgers in the nightcap, Dizzy remarked, "If I'd known Paul was going to pitch a no-hitter, I'd pitched one too."

4. SATCHEL PAIGE

It is estimated that Satchel Paige won more than 2,000 games and pitched more than 100 no-hitters during his long career. Unable to play in the major leagues until 1948 when he was forty-two, Paige once struck out twenty-two major leaguers in an exhibition game and defeated Dizzy Dean four times. Satchel used a wide arsenal of pitches that he gave names like "Long Tom," the bee ball, the trouble ball, and the celebrated hesitation pitch. Paige was a master storyteller and enhanced his legend with tales of his remarkable pitching feats. When he was finally permitted to play in the major leagues in 1948, he demonstrated his control by throwing strikes over a gum wrapper.

5. JOHN "THE COUNT" MONTEFUSCO

John "The Count" Montefusco never lacked confidence. The San Francisco Giants' righthander was National League Rookie of the Year in 1975 and no-hit the Atlanta Braves on September 29, 1976. Once, he guaranteed that he would shut out the Braves and made good his promise. Against the Big Red Machine, the brash rookie boasted that he would shut out Cincinnati and hit a home run. The Count pitched a shutout, hit a home run, and fanned Johnny Bench three times. On July 31, 1975, Montefusco predicted he'd throw another shutout against the Reds and strike out Johnny Bench four times. This time he was shelled for seven runs in two innings, the crushing blow a three-run home run by Bench. Unfazed, the Count revealed that his ultimate fantasy was to be brought to the park in a Rolls Royce and walk to the mound wearing a top hat, cape, and white gloves.

6. JEFFREY LEONARD

Jeffrey Leonard had a knack for irritating the opposition. The outfielder, known as "Penitentiary Face" because of his scowl, showed up pitchers when he hit a home run with his "one flap down" home-run trot (he held one arm against his side). During the 1987 National League Championship series he hit four home runs, taking nearly a minute to round the bases on one homer. Leonard sometimes carried his "nasty" bat to the plate. Obscene words were written on the label, which he waved in the catcher's face.

7. DEION SANDERS

"Neon" Deion Sanders knew how to showboat even as a rookie. He strode to the plate wearing ropes of gold jewelry around his neck. When he hit his first home run, he bent over to tie his shoe when he reached the plate, pointing his rear at the pitcher. Opposing pitchers frequently complained about his baserunning antics.

8. BROADWAY BILL SCHUSTER

Infielder Broadway Bill Schuster would yell at the top of his lungs whenever he got a hit or made a great play. These occurrences were not that frequent, as Broadway Bill only had sixty-one hits in his five-year career, which ended in 1945.

9. GEORGE "SHOWBOAT" FISHER

George Fisher batted .374 in 254 at bats as a rookie outfielder with the St. Louis Cardinals in 1930. The Gas House Gang was one of the most colorful teams in major league history, but Fisher was such a hot dog that he was given the nick-name "Showboat." Despite having one of the highest batting averages in the National League, Fisher was not invited back to play with the Cardinals in 1931. The next season he batted only .182 with the St. Louis Browns and never played in the majors again.

10. JAKE BECKLEY

During his Hall of Fame career, from 1888 to 1907, first baseman Jake Beckley collected nearly 3,000 hits and batted over .300 thirteen times. He intimidated pitchers by pointing his bat at them and letting out a blood-curdling yell, "Chickazoola."

Worst Practical Jokers

For some players, the practical joke has been raised to an art form. From a simple hot foot to elaborate schemes, these pranksters made life miserable for their teammates.

1. MOE DRABOWSKI

Born in Ozanna, Poland, Moe Drabowski pitched in the major leagues for seventeen years. The high point of his career occurred in the first game of the 1966 World Series when the Oriole hurler struck out eleven Dodgers in relief. Drabowski's true claim to fame was his arsenal of practical jokes. While sitting in the bullpen, he might call for fast food or make long-distance calls to check on the weather in foreign cities. While playing Kansas City, he once called the A's bullpen and, while imitating manager Alvin Dark, told someone to start throwing. Starter Jim Nash, who was pitching a shutout, was so unnerved that he lost the game. While pitching for Kansas City, he imitated Charlie Finley and carried on bogus contract negotiations with players.

Drabowski put sneezing powder in the Orioles' air-conditioning system and a goldfish in the water cooler. On another occasion, he sent Chico Salmon a box with a boa constrictor in it. Other teammates found snakes in their locker. At a sports banquet, Brooks Robinson nearly had a heart attack when he discovered a king snake in a basket of dinner rolls.

Many of Moe's teammates were victims of the old hot foot tricks. He would let out the air in their tires or put limburger cheese in their cars. Drabowski was especially fond of throwing smoke bombs in showers and placing firecrackers in inappropriate places. His most outrageous moment came when he gave Baseball Commissioner Bowie Kuhn a hotfoot.

2. DANNY GARDELLA

Danny "Tarzan" Gardella was a power-hitting outfielder with the New York Giants during World War II. He successfully challenged baseball's reserve clause after being suspended for five years after jumping to the Mexican League. Gardella was notorious for his sometimes cruel practical jokes.

On V-E Day he dressed up like Hitler and convinced some that the Fuhrer was not dead. He told teammate Nap Reyes that he was considering suicide. Reyes heard a scream from his hotel room and rushed in to see the window open. Reyes, believing that Gardella had jumped twenty stories to his death, rushed to the window only to find him huddled on the ledge.

3. RABBIT MARANVILLE

One of baseball's biggest clowns, Hall of Fame shortstop Rabbit Maranville played in the major leagues from 1912 to 1935. Maranville like to put a pair of glasses on an umpire after a bad call. His idea of a good joke was to dangle teammates out of the hotel room windows. One night teammates heard Maranville shout that someone was trying to kill him, followed by a gunshot. Frantically, they broke the door down only to be greeted by a smiling Rabbit.

4. JAY JOHNSTONE

Jay Johnstone played twenty seasons in the majors, mainly as a part-time player. In 1980, the Los Angeles Dodgers acquired him because manager Tommy Lasorda believed the outfielder would help keep the team loose. Lasorda became the main target for his hijinks. During spring training,

Johnstone disconnected Lasorda's phone and tied the door of his room to a palm tree so he couldn't get out. With the help of his accomplice, pitcher Jerry Reuss, Johnstone removed the manager's prized photographs of his celebrity friends and replaced them with photos of Johnstone and Reuss. Players were also targets of Johnstone's chicanery. He put a melted brownie in Steve Garvey's glove and made it appear that Reuss had been the culprit.

5. ROGER MCDOWELL

During the late 1980s, Roger McDowell was the ace of the New York Mets' bullpen. He was also among the league leaders in practical jokes. McDowell placed firecrackers in the bat rack and shaving cream on the bullpen phone. Players routinely received the hot foot treatment courtesy of McDowell. Roger accumulated an extensive collection of masks—each to mimic another player or coach.

6. RICK DEMPSEY

Catcher Rick Dempsey played twenty seasons in the major leagues. A clutch hitter, his best moments came in the World Series in which he batted .324. Dempsey's practical jokes usually bordered on the dangerous. Once, when a group of his teammates were playing poker, Dempsey turned out the lights and imitated a robber who threatened to kill them if they didn't give him all their money. Dempsey's lasting contribution to the game may have been his headfirst slides on the tarp during rain delays while imitating Babe Ruth.

7. JOE PAGE

Yankees' reliever Joe Page devised one of the most famous practical jokes at the expense of teammate Snuffy Stirnweiss. Page propped a bear carcass on an outhouse toilet seat. Unsuspectingly, Snuffy opened the door only to have the bear fall over and pin him to the ground.

8. BO BELINSKY

Next to women, practical jokes were Bo Belinsky's favorite pastime. Bo promised to line up a teammate with a beautiful woman. The date turned out to be a drag queen. He gave another player the phone number of what he promised would be a dream date. The number actually belonged to crusty manager Bill Rigney. In the minors Bo and fellow hellraiser Steve Dalkowski learned that Miss Universe was staying in the adjoining suite. To get a better look, they drilled holes in the hotel wall.

9. **ARLIE LATHAM**

No one was safe when Arlie Latham was around. He tormented fans, teammates, rivals, and even owners with his shenanigans. He put on a bulbous nose and did a devastating impression of owner Chris Von der Ahe. John McGraw selected him to be the first third base coach. A gifted acrobat, Latham once somersaulted over manager Cap Anson and occasionally cartwheeled down the third base line when he sent a runner home.

10. **BERT BLYLEVEN**

Bert Blyleven won 287 games and struck out 3,701 batters during his outstanding career, which ended in 1992. Blyleven had a puckish sense of humor and was the undisputed king of the hotfoot. He attributed the secret to his outstanding curve ball to his long fingers. Born in Holland, Blyleven said the length of his fingers were the results of sticking them in dikes as a child.

Flakes

In baseball, a flake is someone whose behavior deviates from the norm. Meet some of baseball's biggest oddballs.

1. RUBE WADDELL

Blessed with a blazing fastball and sharp breaking curve, Rube Waddell led the league in strikeouts seven times between 1900 and 1907. The child-like pitcher would sometimes hold up the start of a game in order to play marbles with kids in the street. He was known to bolt off the mound and chase fire engines (at the age of three he had run away from home and was found sleeping in a fire-house). Opposing players could distract him by waving stuffed animals from the dugout.

Rube once jumped out a second-story window because he believed he could fly. Despite being one of the best pitchers in baseball, he never

Jackie Brandt
It is believed that the term flake was coined to describe the behavior of out-fielder Jackie Brandt.

earned more than $2,800 in a season. The A's paid him in dollar bills because they believed it would help Rube make it last longer. During the off-season he earned extra money by wrestling alligators in Florida. Waddell died on April Fools' Day, 1914, at the age of thirty-seven.

2. BILL "SPACEMAN" LEE

Bill Lee was a good enough pitcher to win seventeen games for three consecutive seasons from 1973 to 1975. Nicknamed "Spaceman," the zany southpaw claimed he was normal, and it was the "northpaw" outlook on life that was strange. Lee admitted to sprinkling marijuana on his organic buckwheat pancakes. When he was fined $250 for the remark, he donated the money to an Eskimo charity. In Boston he wore the number 37 (which had been Jimmy Piersall's number) and asked if he could change it to 337 because the numbers would spell Lee upside down.

It was Lee who dubbed manager Don Zimmer the "Gerbil." He formed a group of players called the Loyal Order of the Buffalo Heads that mocked Zimmer. Boston City Councilor Albert O'Neil wrote Lee an angry letter with some misspelled words after Lee had called Boston a racist city. Lee wrote back a nice letter warning the city official that some idiot was using his stationery. The Spaceman read books by mystics and believed that the perfect pitcher would be a Tibetan priest who could make the ball disappear and reappear in the catcher's mitt. Lee authored an autobiography entitled *The Wrong Stuff* and ran for president on the Rhinoceros Party ticket.

3. MARK "THE BIRD" FIDRYCH

Mark Fidrych was working at a gas station when he was signed by the Detroit Tigers. The twenty-one-year-old pitcher surprised everyone by being called up to the majors in 1976. He celebrated his promotion by making love to his girlfriend on the pitching mound.

Fidrych was an immediate sensation, pitching a two-hitter in his first start. He won nineteen games as a rookie and led the American League in earned run average. Baseball had never seen anything like him. Fidrych got down on his hands and knees to manicure the mound. He talked to the ball and shook hands with his infielders. If a batter got a base hit, he refused to use the same ball again. After he got a batter out he would walk around the mound like a bird and occasionally flap his arms.

For a season "The Bird" was the word in Detroit. After a win, Fidrych would do a lap of the field waving to fans. One game he was warming up when he realized he had forgot to wear his protective cup. Totally uninhibited, he pulled down his pants and put on his cup. With his long blonde curls, he was a favorite of female fans. When he went to the barber shop, groupies would rush in and sweep up the golden locks. Sadly, "The Bird" injured his wing the following season and won only ten more major league games.

4. SUPER JOE CHARBONEAU

Like Fidrych, Joe Charboneau was a one-year wonder. In 1980, Charboneau was Rookie of the Year when he hit twenty-three home runs for the

Cleveland Indians. Super Joe seemed like some-one out of *Animal House*. He dyed his hair different colors years before Dennis Rodman did. On a dare, he drank a bottle of beer through his nose. Charboneau frequently abused his body when doing stunts. He opened a bottle of beer with his eyesocket, cut away a tattoo, and even removed a tooth. He underwent two back operations and played in only seventy games after his rookie season.

5. FRENCHY BORDAGARAY

Frenchy Bordagaray was an outstanding pinch hitter during the 1930s and 1940s. Frenchy was a manager's nightmare. While chasing a fly ball, he lost his cap. Bordagaray went back and picked up his cap before renewing his quest for the ball. Another time he was chastised by manager Casey Stengel for not sliding. The next time he hit a home run, Frenchy slid into every base to show that he had learned his lesson.

6. JACKIE BRANDT

Some believe that the term "flake" derived from a teammate commenting on Jackie Brandt, "Things seem to flake off his mind and disappear." Brandt played outfield in the majors from 1956 to 1967. Questioned about his intensity before the 1962 season, Brandt promised, "This year I'm going to play with harder nonchalance." He blamed his inconsistent defensive play on the fact that when he ran hard, his eyeballs jumped up and down.

7. JIM COLBORN

Jim Colborn's best season was 1973, when he won twenty games for the Milwaukee Brewers. He also pitched a no-hitter against the Texas Rangers in 1977. A master of impersonation, he disguised himself as an umpire, groundskeeper, peanut vendor, batboy, and even as a mascot. If only he could have impersonated Jim Palmer.

8. GEORGE STALLINGS

If there was ever a manager (other than Casey Stengel) who was a flake, it was George Stallings. He managed the 1914 Boston Braves to one of the greatest comebacks in baseball history. In last place on the Fourth of July, the Miracle Braves rallied to win fifty-two of their sixty-six games to capture the pennant. Tremendously superstitious, he physically froze during a rally and would not move until the inning was over. He shook bats to "wake up" the lumber. Stallings believed loose paper or peanut shells on the floor of the dugout was bad luck, and opposing managers had players shred newspapers to annoy him. The manager was given the nickname "Bonehead" because that was what he frequently called his players.

9. **RICK BOSETTI**

Rick Bosetti was an outfielder of modest talent who played from 1976 to 1982. His legacy to the game was his ambition to urinate in the outfield of every stadium, a goal that he achieved.

10. **KEITH RHOMBERG**

Keith Rhomberg was an outfielder with the Cleveland Indians from 1982 to 1984. Despite a .383 lifetime batting average, he played in only forty-one games. One of his drawbacks was that for him, life was a game of tag. Whenever someone touched him, he insisted that he touch him back. A teammate tagged him with the ball and threw it over the outfield fence, prompting Rhomberg to frantically climb over the fence to retrieve the ball. Fans wrote taunting letters, to which he always replied because they had touched them last. Finally, opposing players began bumping against Rhomberg and were chased all over the field by the superstitious player. Thank God, he didn't play football.

The Bullpen

For some reason, relief pitchers have a tendency to be bigger flakes than players at other positions. Maybe it's because they have too much time on their hands in the bullpen.

1. BILL FAUL

Bill Faul attended the University of Cincinnati and broke Sandy Koufax's school record when he struck out nineteen batters in a game. He later set an NCAA record when he fanned twenty-four. Although no Koufax, Faul pitched in the majors from 1962 to 1970. After experiencing modest success as a starter, Faul was moved to the bullpen where he won only one more game. He held a degree as a doctor of divinity and had been a karate instructor in the Air Force. He practiced karate, and he also preached for the Universal

Christian Church. A licensed hypnotist, he hyp-
notized himself prior to each game. Before pitching to a batter, Faul waved his hand in front of his
face. Considering his 12–16 lifetime record, he
should have tried hypnotizing the batters.

2. JIM KERN

Jim Kern, despite control problems, had a sensational season with Texas in 1979, saving twenty-
nine games and posting a 1.57 earned run average. Kern once told sportswriters he was working
on a new pitch—a strike. The Texas bullpen was
known as the "Cuckoo's Nest," and Kern was
nicknamed "Emu" because he looked like a big
bird. When fans in the stands asked for a ball,
Kern not only obliged them, he tossed them his
glove, cap, uniform, and socks. Another time
Kern came out on the field wearing his uniform
backwards.

3. AL HRABOSKY

Al "The Mad Hungarian" Hrabosky was a splendid
reliever who compiled a 64–35 record during his
career, which ended in 1982. The only thing better than his pitching was his act. Hrabosky would
stomp in from the bullpen while the organist
played "The Hungarian Rhapsody." The Mad
Hungarian would psyche himself while rubbing up

the ball. He was an intimidating sight with his Fu Manchu mustache and long hair. Hrabosky wore a Gypsy Rose of Death ring to ward off werewolves. Atlanta Braves' owner Ted Turner was so impressed that he signed him to an unprecedented thirty-year contract.

4. BRAD LESLEY

For a pitcher who won only one major league game, Brad "The Animal" Lesley left a lasting impression. Lesley pitched in the big leagues from 1982 to 1985. An imposing pitcher who stood 6 feet 6 inches and weighed 230 pounds, he would grunt and clench his fists every time he struck out a batter (which wasn't that often since he had forty-six career K's). The real strikeout king, Nolan Ryan, once imitated his act when he struck out a batter against Cincinnati.

5. TURK WENDELL

When Turk Wendell came up with the Chicago Cubs, he went through a series of rituals during each mound appearance. Turk waved to the center-fielder before each inning and insisted that the ball be rolled to him. Wendell made three crosses in the dirt. He always chewed licorice and wore two watches (one with the current time at his home in Massachusetts). When Turk walked to the dugout, he leaped over the foul line. Wendell wore uniform number 13, probably to prove that he wasn't superstitious.

6. TUG MCGRAW

Tug McGraw was an outstanding reliever who pitched with the Mets and Phillies between 1965 and 1984. Tom Seaver once said that McGraw only had forty-eight cards in his deck. Tug expressed a dislike for Astroturf because he didn't want to play on anything he couldn't smoke. McGraw gave his pitches names. He called his fastball Peggy Lee—Is That All There Is? Cutty Sark was a pitch that sailed. The Bo Derek was one "with a nice little tail on it." When asked what he did with a bonus, Tug replied, "I spent half of it on booze and broads. The other half I wasted."

7. LARRY ANDERSEN

Larry Andersen had a major league career that spanned three decades, from the 1970s to the 1990s. Andersen was the Steven Wright of baseball. He pondered such matters as why slim chance and fat chance meant the same thing, and how do you know when invisible ink is dry? While with the Phillies he sprayed on "instant hair" out of an aerosol can to significantly lower his hairline. Andersen will always be remembered as the man for whom the Red Sox traded Jeff Bagwell.

8. **ROB DIBBLE**

The nastiest of the "Nasty Boys" relievers that led the 1990 Cincinnati Reds to a world championship, Rob Dibble had more suspensions than Albert Belle. The man with the 100-mile per hour fastball was suspended for throwing at batter Eric Yelding, throwing at the legs of runner Doug Dascenzo, and hitting a fan with a ball he threw into the centerfield stands. Dibble refused to shake hands or sign more than a few autographs because he was afraid to hurt his arm. In 1994, he suffered a career-ending rotator cuff injury.

9. **DON STANHOUSE**

Don Stanhouse, a reliever in the major leagues from 1972 to 1982, earned the nickname "Stan the Man Unusual." Baltimore manager Earl Weaver called him "Full Pack" because he could smoke a pack of cigarettes by the time his reliever could finish the game. Stanhouse liked to hang upside down in the bullpen—a habit terminated when he fell on his head.

10. **BILLY LOES**

Billy Loes was one of the mainstays of the Brooklyn Dodgers' staff in the early 1950s. When he was a starter he declared that he didn't want to win twenty games because management would expect it every year. When he booted a ball hit back to the mound, the resourceful Loes explained that he had lost it in the sun.

Curses

You may not believe in them, but curses seemed to have had a major impact on baseball. You are about to enter baseball's twilight zone.

1. THE CURSE OF THE BAMBINO

Led by Babe Ruth, the best left-handed pitcher in the American League, the Boston Red Sox were the dominant team of the teens. Despite the team's success, Boston's owner Harry Frazee was strapped for cash to finance his new Broadway musical. He sold his star pitcher and part-time outfielder to the New York Yankees in 1920 for $100,000. With the Yankees, Ruth became the greatest slugger ever to play the game. The Red Sox, who had won five world championships and were baseball's dominant team, have never won another World Series. In contrast, the Yankees became the most successful franchise in sports history. By the way, the play Frazee produced with the money from the Yankees was "No, No, Nanette."

2. THE BILLY GOAT CURSE

For more than fifty years the Chicago Cubs have personified futility in major league baseball. In 1945, tavern owner William Sianis found a goat wandering the streets of Chicago. Apparently, the animal had fallen from a livestock truck. Sianis took the goat home and made it his pet. They were inseparable, and when he decided to take the goat with him to the fourth game of the 1945 World Series between the Cubs and the Detroit Tigers, the ushers at Wrigley Field refused to let Sianis enter the ballpark with his pet. Outraged, he shouted, "The Cubs will never win another pennant." And to this day, they haven't.

3. THE EX-CUB CURSE

The only thing worse than a Cub is an ex-Cub. Since 1945, the year the Cubs won their last pennant, only one team with three or more ex-Cubs has won a World Series. The only team to overcome the curse was the 1960 Pittsburgh Pirates, who somehow managed to win the series against the New York Yankees despite being outscored, 55–27. Teams with a surplus of ex-Cubs have a 1–13 record in the fall classic. The ex-Cub curse

became well known in 1990 when Chicago columnist Mike Royko guaranteed that the heavily
favored Oakland A's would lose to the Cincinnati
Reds because they had the curse of having three
ex-Cubs on their roster. The Reds swept the star-
studded A's in four games.

4. PEDRO BORBON

Reliever Pedro Borbon was the wild man of the
Big Red Machine teams in Cincinnati that dominated baseball in the 1970s. On one occasion an
opposing player was forced to get a tetanus shot
after Borbon bit him. When Pedro was traded to
San Francisco in 1979, he placed a voodoo curse
on the Reds, swearing that they would never win
another pennant. Within a few years, the Reds
had plummeted to the National League cellar. In
1990, Borbon agreed to lift the curse, and the
Reds won their first pennant since he left.

5. THE CURSE OF THE ANGELS

Anaheim Stadium, home of the Anaheim Angels,
was built in 1966 on the burial grounds of the
Gabrieleño Indians. The Angels have experienced
the worst luck of any team in baseball. While the
ballpark was being built, pitcher Dick Wentz died
of a brain tumor. In 1972, utility player Chico Ruiz
was killed in an automobile accident. Five years
later, promising shortstop Mike Miley met the

same fate. The next season, star outfielder Lyman Bostock was shot to death in a case of mistaken identity. The Angels' luck appeared to be changing when they were on the verge of defeating the Boston Red Sox in the 1986 American League championship series when reliever Donnie Moore gave up a home run to Dave Henderson that turned the tide. The Angels lost the series and have never won a pennant. Three years later, Moore, despondent over surrendering the home run, took his own life.

6. FREDDY KAHAULUA

Pitcher Freddy Kahaulua had his own curse when he arrived in Angels' training camp in 1977. He was unable to lift his pitching arm. Kahaulua explained that his ex-girlfriend's mother in Hawaii had put a curse on him that prevented him from lifting his left arm. Desperate to find a solution, club officials contacted the woman, and she agreed to lift the curse. Immediately, Kahaulua was able to lift his arm and to pitch again.

7. BOB OJEDA

In July 1991, Los Angeles pitcher Bob Ojeda was shelled against the New York Mets, losing the game 9–4. He told reporters after the game that his poor performance was the result of voodoo. Ojeda explained that his ex-wife, with whom he was involved in a alimony dispute, had been sticking pins in a voodoo doll with Ojeda's face on it.

8. MIKE CUELLAR

Pitcher Mike Cuellar was a Cy Young winner who won 185 games in his career, which lasted from 1958 to 1977. In order to keep evil spirits out of his hotel room, the four-time twenty game winner stuffed paper in keyholes and under doors.

9. LEO CARDENAS

Leo Cardenas was a top shortstop during his major league career, which lasted from 1960 to 1975. A firm believer in the powers of voodoo, he had a collection of dolls dressed in other teams' uniforms. Cardenas prepared potions and went through a series of rituals before a game. Whenever he went into a hitting slump, he punished his bats by locking them in his car trunk.

10. JOSE RIJO

Cincinnati Reds pitcher Jose Rijo was the Most Valuable Player in the 1990 World Series. Rijo kept a voodoo doll in his locker, along with a picture of Pope John Paul II. When he pitched, he hung the photo of the Pope on the wall. He reasoned that he would lose only if the photo fell off the wall.

Lucky Bounces

Sometimes it's better to be lucky than good. Luck paid a pivotal role in the careers of these individuals.

1. CHARLES "VICTORY" FAUST

Pitcher Charlie Faust never won a game in the major leagues, but he helped the New York Giants win three pennants. In 1911, he approached manager John McGraw and said that a fortune teller had predicted that he would pitch for the Giants, and that they would win the pennant. Believing he might be good luck, McGraw let Faust suit up for the games.

Faust warmed up on the sidelines almost every game. It seemed as though every time he warmed up, the Giants had a big inning. Perhaps the players felt they needed insurance runs just in case Faust was ever brought into the game. McGraw did permit Faust to pitch two innings in which he gave up one run. As the fortune teller predicted, the Giants won the pennant in 1911. Faust became a popular attraction in vaudeville, telling audiences how he had clinched the pennant for New York. In both 1912 and 1913, the Giants experienced long losing streaks. McGraw summoned Faust, and the Giants went on to win the pennant both seasons. Faust's mental problems became more serious, and he was institutionalized. Without their good luck charm, the Giants finished ten games behind the Miracle Braves. On June 18, 1915, Faust's luck ran out, and he died at the age of thirty-four. The Giants finished last that season. A strange twist on the Faust legend.

2. JACK "LUCKY" LOHRKE

Jack Lohrke was an infielder in the major leagues from 1947 to 1953. The real story is that he survived long enough to play in the major leagues. During World War II he was part of the Normandy invasion and fought at the Battle of the Bulge. Four times, soldiers on both sides of him were killed, but Lohrke came through the war unscathed. When the war ended, Lohrke was scheduled to fly home in an army transport plane. He was bumped from the flight at the last minute, and the plane crashed, killing everyone on board. In 1946, Lohrke was playing minor league baseball with the Spokane Indians, when he was told to report to San Diego. He got off the team bus in Ellensburg, Washington. Fifteen minutes later the bus crashed into a ravine in the Cascade Mountains, killing nine players.

3. EDDIE BENNETT

Eddie Bennett was born with a deformed spine. He became a batboy for the 1919 Chicago White Sox. Outfielder Happy Felsch, who would become one of the players banned for life in the Black Sox scandal, would rub Bennett's hunchback for good luck. The White Sox won the pennant. The next season, Bennett became batboy for the Brooklyn Dodgers, and they, too, won the pennant. In 1921, Bennett moved to the Yankees, who won their first pennant. With Bennett in the dugout, the New York Yankees became a dynasty.

4. L'IL RASTUS

Rastus was a black youth discovered sleeping in a park by Ty Cobb. For some reason Cobb, an avid racist, believed the teenager was a good luck charm. For most of the 1908 season, the Tigers' players insisted on rubbing their fingers through Rastus's hair before going to the plate. When Detroit began losing late in the season, Rastus was let go by the Tigers. He turned up with

Chicago, and the Cubs defeated Detroit in the World Series, their last world championship. The next season Rastus returned to Detroit, and they won the pennant.

5. GOOSE GOSLIN

Rather than use a rabbit's foot as a good luck charm, Detroit outfielder Goose Goslin decided a live rabbit would be better. He kept a rabbit in the clubhouse during the 1935 World Series against the Chicago Cubs. Goslin's single in the ninth inning drove in the winning run in the sixth and deciding game.

6. BO BELINKSY

On the night before he threw his no-hitter against Baltimore, Angels pitcher Bo Belinsky stayed out until 4 A.M. with a comely blonde. Belinsky considered her to be his good luck charm, but no matter how hard he tried to locate her, he never saw her again.

7. VIDA BLUE

Three times during the 1970s, lefthander Vida Blue won twenty games for the Oakland A's. He insisted on wearing his lucky cap, which became discolored by sweat and dirt. On April 16, 1977, he was forced to discard the lucky hat because it

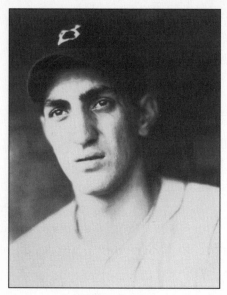

Ralph Branca
During the fateful 1951 season, Brooklyn
pitcher Ralph Branca wore number 13
on his uniform and won 13 games.

no longer conformed with the uniforms of his
teammates. Blue led the American League in
losses in 1977 and was traded to San Francisco.

8. DON STANHOUSE

Don Stanhouse was pitching for the Los Angeles
Dodgers when he was given a stuffed monkey.
Stanhouse brought the monkey to the clubhouse,
and the Dodgers went on a winning streak. The
monkey became Stanhouse's constant compan-
ion, even sharing beers to celebrate victories.

9. SUNSET JIMMY BURKE

Jimmy Burke played third base for five different teams between 1899 and 1905. He earned the nickname "Sunset" because he believed it was unlucky to eat dinner before the sun went down.

10. RALPH BRANCA

Brooklyn pitcher Ralph Branca seemed to be tempting fate when he posed for a photograph prior to the 1951 season. Branca, who wore number 13, posed with a black cat. He won thirteen games that season, then gave up Bobby Thomson's "Shot Heard Round the World" in the play-offs, which gave the Giants the pennant.

The Meat of the Order

Ballplayers sometimes use their meal money for strange things. Ron LeFlore was nicknamed the "Bosco Bear" because of his favorite beverage. Brett Butler was known to drink up to twenty cups of coffee before a game and was rarely caught napping on the basepaths. Denny McLain drank more than 100 bottles of Pepsi a week in his prime. Baltimore reliever Dick Hall once ate a seventeen-year cicada. See what's on the menu.

1. WADE BOGGS

Five-time batting champion Wade Boggs attributed much of his success to eating chicken. For nine years he ate nothing but chicken. Boggs chose from a thirteen-recipe rotation. Lemon chicken became a special favorite after Boggs rapped out seven hits in a doubleheader in 1982.

2. RUSTY STAUB

Rusty Staub retired in 1985 with 2,716 base hits. Nicknamed "Le Grand Orange" when he played in Montreal because of his red hair, the New Orleans native had the reputation of being a food and wine connoisseur. In August 1997, Staub served as a celebrity chef at the Trois Jean Bistro in New York. The menu included family recipes such as Soft Shell Crab Amandine and Shrimp Stuffed Eggplant.

3. PING BODIE

Ping Bodie was an outfielder in the American League from 1911 to 1921. During spring training in 1919, Bodie, who was playing for the Yankees, challenged an ostrich to a spaghetti eating contest. The epic encounter ended when the ostrich keeled over.

4. TOMMY LASORDA

In between diets, former Dodgers' manager Tommy Lasorda performed prodigious feats of eating. In one pregame meal in 1986, Lasorda won a bet by eating 100 oysters.

5. YOGI BERRA

When asked if he wanted his pizza sliced into four or eight pieces, Yogi replied, "Better make it four.

I don't think I can eat eight." The weight-conscious catcher once told a waitress, "I'll have some French fries, but no potatoes because I'm on a diet." Yogi once asked the clubhouse man to bring him a diet Tab.

6. BABE RUTH

Waite Hoyt said of Babe Ruth, "If you cut that big slop in half, most of the concessions of Yankees Stadium would come pouring out." For breakfast, Babe was known to eat chocolate ice cream washed down by beer, whiskey, and ginger ale.

7. JIMMIE FOXX

On July 3, 1940, slugger Jimmie Foxx was offered a dozen lobsters by a fan if he hit a home run. Foxx won the bet and ate all twelve lobsters in one sitting. Tragically, he choked to death on a piece of meat in 1967.

8. BEN MCDONALD

Louisiana native Ben McDonald swears that his favorite dish is squirrel head. He says that he finds the brain and tongue especially tasty.

9. MICKEY TETTLETON

Mickey Tettleton began his long and successful major league career with Oakland in 1984. In

1989, the catcher belted twenty-six home runs with Baltimore, fifteen more than he had ever hit in a season. He attributed his power surge to eating Fruit Loops cereal.

10. **TOMMY BURNS**

Tommy Burns played every position during his years in the majors from 1884 to 1895. A .301 career hitter, he was given the nickname "Oyster" because of the large number of oysters that he ate before each game. During the off-season, Burns made a living selling shellfish.

Fat Tubs of Goo

Baseball players come in all sizes. These players are of the extra large variety. Learn more about baseball's heavy hitters.

1. WALTER "JUMBO" BROWN

Jumbo Brown was the heaviest player in major league history, tipping the scales at nearly 300 pounds. The hefty hurler was good enough to lead the National League in saves in 1940 and 1941. Jumbo was so enormous that the Yankees billed him as the "man who swallowed a taxi cab."

2. TERRY FORSTER

Terry Forster pitched sixteen years in the majors and led the American League in saves in 1974. Unlike most relief pitchers, Forster was an excellent hitter, compiling a lifetime batting average of .397. In June 1985, he became immortalized when David Letterman described him as a "fat tub of goo." Forster, who weighted nearly 270 pounds, appeared on the program carrying seven hot dogs, a triple decker, two cans of Coke, and a candy bar. The reliever, capitalizing on his fame, made a music video entitled "Fat Is In." Forster joked, "A waist is a terrible thing to mind."

3. CHARLIE KERFELD

Twenty-two-year-old reliever Charlie Kerfeld was 11–2 with the Houston Astros in 1986. The only thing Kerfeld liked to do more than win was to eat. In July 1987, he was caught eating a plate of ribs in the bullpen during a game. As his weight ballooned past 250 pounds, he became less effective as a pitcher. Kerfeld didn't win another game and was out of baseball at age twenty-three. Charlie admitted that the only thing that intimidated him was a scale.

4. GARLAND BUCKEYE

Known as the "Pitching Pachyderm," Garland Buckeye had a 30–39 record in a career that ran from 1918 to 1928. The 260-pounder played guard for the NFL Cardinals from 1921 to 1924.

5. FATS FOTHERGILL

Bob "Fats" Fothergill batted over .300 his first eight seasons and retired in 1933 with a .326 batting average. Fothergill always seemed to hit .300

and weighed nearly as much. The overweight outfielder had a reputation for busting outfield fences while chasing fly balls. He once bit umpire Bill Dinneen during an argument. Fats, at the time in the midst of a crash diet, confessed, "That was the first bite of meat I had in a month."

6. DON ROBINSON

Don Robinson won fourteen games for Pittsburgh in 1978 and was voted the National League Rookie Pitcher of the Year. Concerned with Robinson's weight, management inserted an incentive clause that would pay him an extra $100,000 if he stayed below 225 pounds. Robinson renegotiated his contract to raise his weight limit to 235.

7. GATES BROWN

Pinch hitter extraordinaire Gates Brown batted .370 for the 1968 World Champion Detroit Tigers. On August 7, 1968, the Tigers were playing Cleveland when Brown was summoned to pinch hit. Caught by surprise, he was about to eat two hot dogs. Trying to conceal them from the manager, Brown stuffed them in his jersey. Brown hit a double and went into second head first. When he got up, Brown had mustard, catsup, and pieces of buns and wieners all over his uniform.

8. SHANTY HOGAN

James Hogan was a hard-hitting catcher who played from 1925 to 1937. The 240-pounder was nicknamed "Shanty" because he was shaped like a hut.

9. FAT FREDDIE GLADDING

Nicknamed the "Bear" and "Fat Freddie" because of his portly physique, Gladding was a solid reliever for thirteen seasons. He led the National League in saves while with Houston in 1969. Arguably the worst hitter in baseball history, he made only one hit in 450 games for a lifetime .016 average.

10. BOOG POWELL

Big Boog Powell slammed 339 home runs during his career, primarily with the Baltimore Orioles. He was the American League Most Valuable Player in 1970. Manager Frank Robinson once threatened to fine him $1,000 for every pound he weighed over 265. After an eating binge, his weight had soared to nearly 275. Today, Powell runs a successful barbecued ribs concession just beyond the right field stands in Baltimore's Camden Yards.

Graybeards

Life begins at forty for some players. Minnesota's Paul Molitor was forty years old when he led the American League with 225 hits in 1996. Phil Niekro of the Atlanta Braves led the National League with twenty-one wins in 1979 at the age of forty. Both Warren Spahn and Nolan Ryan pitched no-hitters after they turned forty. Impressive as these feats are, these players were in the prime compared to the players you are about to meet.

1. SATCHEL PAIGE

Satchel Paige was the oldest rookie in baseball history when he was signed by the Cleveland Indians in 1948. On September 25, 1965, the fifty-nine-year-old Paige pitched three scoreless innings for Kansas City against the Boston Red Sox to

Hoyt Wilhelm
Reliever Hoyt Wilhelm did not pitch in the major leagues until he was 28 years old and was 49 when he retired in 1972.

become the oldest player ever to appear in a major league game. Two years later, Satchel pitched an inning for Atlanta in an exhibition game versus AAA farm team Richmond and struck out two. His longevity secrets were revealed in his rules on how to stay young:

1. Avoid fried meats, which angry up the blood.

2. If your stomach disputes you, lie down and pacify it with cool thoughts.

3. Keep the juices flowing by jangling around gently as you move.

4. Go very light on the vices, such as carrying on in society. The social ramble ain't restful.

5. Avoid running at all times.

6. Don't look back. Something might be gaining on you.

Paige said, "Age is a matter of mind over matter. If you don't mind, it doesn't matter."

2. HUB KITTLE

The oldest man to play in a professional baseball game was Hub Kettle, who was sixty-three years old when he pitched an inning for a Class A team in Springfield, Illinois, in 1980.

3. MINNIE MINOSO

Minnie Minoso was nearly thirty when he broke into the major leagues in 1949. He made up for lost time, leading the league at various times in hits, doubles, triples, and stolen bases. On September 12, 1976, the fifty-three-year-old Minoso became the oldest player ever to get a base hit in a major league game. Four years later, he became the second player ever to appear in a major league game in five different decades. In 1990, the sixty-seven-year-old Minoso was scheduled to appear in a game for the Chicago White Sox, but Commissioner Fay Vincent refused to let him play because he felt it was just a ploy to increase attendance.

4. NICK ALTROCK

The other man to play in five different decades was Nick Altrock. He was a twenty-game winner for the Chicago White Stockings in 1905 and 1906. One of baseball's greatest clowns, Altrock appeared in his last game at the age of fifty-seven in 1933 with Washington.

5. PAT JORDAN

Pat Jordan was fifty-six years old when he pitched a scoreless inning for the Waterbury Spirits of the Northeast League on July 29, 1997. Jordan had last pitched professionally thirty-six years earlier for a Class D farm team of the Milwaukee Braves. In the years in between, he had been a success-ful writer, most notably for *Sports Illustrated*.

6. ORATOR JIM O'ROURKE

A graduate of the Yale Law School, Jim O'Rourke got his nickname because of his long-winded ora-tions. A .310 lifetime hitter, he was elected to the Baseball Hall of Fame in 1945. In 1904, the fifty-two-year-old O'Rourke caught a game for the New York Giants and managed to hit a single and score a run. Eight years later, at the age of sixty, he caught an entire game for New Haven of the Connecticut League. O'Rourke was president of the league at the time.

7. JACK QUINN

Spitballer Jack Quinn won 247 games during his twenty-three-year career. He set a number of records for longevity. At age forty-six, he was the oldest pitcher to start a World Series game. When he was forty-seven, he became the oldest to hit a home run. Quinn was forty-nine years old when he became the oldest pitcher to win a major league game. Amazingly, he led the National League in saves with Brooklyn in 1932 when he was forty-nine years old.

8. HOYT WILHELM

Hoyt Wilhelm was the first relief pitcher to be inducted into the Baseball Hall of Fame. As a twenty-eight-year-old rookie in 1952, Wilhelm led the National League in earned run average, winning percentage, and games pitched. By the time he retired at age forty-nine in 1972, Wilhelm had pitched in a record 1,070 games.

9. CAP ANSON

Possibly the greatest player of the nineteenth century, Cap Anson played twenty-two seasons in

Chicago. In his final major league game on October 3, 1897, forty-five-year-old Anson belted two home runs.

10. CONNIE MACK

In 1950, fifty-six years after he managed his first major league game, Connie Mack, a few months shy of his eighty-eighth birthday, retired as manager of the Philadelphia Athletics.

Playing Young

Dwight Gooden won seventeen games for the Mets as a nineteen-year-old in 1984. All of the players in this chapter had major league experience before their eighteenth birthday.

1. JOE NUXHALL

Joe Nuxhall was a fifteen-year-old high school student in Hamilton, Ohio when he was signed to pitch for the Cincinnati Reds. On June 10, 1944, Nuxhall became the youngest player in major league history when he entered the game trailing 13–0 against the defending world champion St. Louis Cardinals. Nuxhall retired the first two batters, then gave up five runs on five walks and two hits. His earned run average for the game was an astronomical 67.50. Nuxhall recalled that he had been pitching to junior high students three weeks earlier and suddenly he's facing Stan Musial. He didn't pitch in the majors for another eight years, but eventually won 135 games.

2. CARL SCHEIB

Carl Scheib was another high school student pressed into major league action during World War II. On September 6, 1943, the sixteen-year-old became the youngest player in American League history when he pitched in a game for the Philadelphia Athletics. Although he pitched eleven years in the big leagues, Scheib was finished by the time he was twenty-seven.

3. JIM DERRINGTON

Sixteen-year-old Jim Derrington was the youngest player in the twentieth century to start a major league game. In 1956, he started for the Chicago White Sox, giving up five runs in six innings. Derrington never won a game and was out of the majors at the age of seventeen.

4. JOE RELFORD

Joe Relford, a twelve-year-old bat boy, was the youngest person ever to appear in a minor league baseball game. On July 19, 1952, Relford was put into a Class D game by Fitzgeralds' manager

Charlie Ridgeway as a lark in a hopelessly lost game. Relford grounded out but later made a great catch in the outfield. The manager and the umpire who permitted Relford to pinch hit were fired.

5. WILLIE MCGILL

Willie McGill was only sixteen years old when he won eleven games for Cleveland of the Players' League in 1890. McGill won twenty games as a seventeen-year-old, the youngest player ever to reach that milestone, but he was washed up by the age of twenty-two.

6. TOMMY BROWN

Tommy Brown was sixteen years old when he became the starting shortstop for the Brooklyn Dodgers in 1944. Nicknamed "Buckshot," he threw so erratically that the grounds crew sometimes placed the batting cage behind first base to protect the fans. At age seventeen, he became the youngest player to hit a home run in the majors.

7. ROGERS HORNSBY MCKEE

Rogers Hornsby McKee was sixteen years old when he pitched for the Philadelphia Phillies in 1943. McKee won only one game and was only seventeen years old when he pitched his last game in the majors.

8. BOB FELLER

Bob Feller was seventeen years old when he was brought up by Cleveland in 1936. In his major league debut, "Rapid Robert" struck out fifteen St. Louis Browns. Later that season he fanned seventeen Philadelphia A's in a game. Unlike many baseball prodigies, Feller went on to a long and successful career, winning 266 games.

9. MEL OTT

Another early bloomer, Mel Ott was only seventeen when he broke in with the New York Giants in 1926. In his first two seasons, Ott hit only one home run, but by the time he retired in 1947, he had set a National League record with 511 round trippers.

10. JAY DAHL

The Houston Astros made history when they started an all-rookie lineup in a game against the New York Mets on September 27, 1963. The team included future stars Joe Morgan, Rusty Staub, and Jimmy Wynn. The starting pitcher was seventeen-year-old Jay Dahl, who was knocked out of the box in the third inning of the 10–3 loss. Dahl never appeared in another major league game. On June 20, 1965, the nineteen-year-old was killed in an automobile accident, making him the youngest player with major league experience to die.

Minor League Phenoms

Minor league stardom doesn't always insure major league success. Each of these players were minor league sensations but had minor big league careers. Some never made it to the major leagues at all.

1. JOE BAUMAN

The unidentified flying objects over Roswell, New Mexico, in 1954 probably came off the bat of Joe Bauman. Playing for the Roswell Rockets in 1954, Bauman blasted 72 home runs and drove home 224 runs. His 72 homers and .916 slugging percentage are professional baseball records. Despite a .337 career batting average and 337 home runs, Bauman played only one game above Class A ball.

2. STEVE DALKOWSKI

Ted Williams, perhaps the greatest hitter of all time, proclaimed that Steve Dalkowski was the fastest pitcher he had ever seen. Unfortunately, he was also the wildest. During his nine-year career, Dalkowski walked 12.3 batters every nine innings. In 1957, he walked over two batters per inning. One of his high hard ones tore off a batter's ear lobe. Another fastball knocked the umpire twenty feet backwards. Not even the spectators were safe. A Dalkowski pitch was thrown so hard that it went through the screen behind home plate. He once pitched a one-hitter and lost 9–8. In 1959, he allowed forty-one hits in eighty-four innings and struck out 142 batters. The bad news is that he walked 190. He once fanned Joe Pepitone five times in one game. Just when it appeared that he had finally conquered his wildness and might reach the majors, he injured his arm.

3. RON NECCIAI

Ron Necciai pitched the most overpowering game in professional baseball history. On May 13, 1952, "Rocket" Ron struck out twenty-seven batters in a nine-inning no-hitter versus Welch. While pitching for Bristol in the Class C Appalachian League, he allowed only two hits and struck out seventy-seven in thirty-one innings. Rushed to the majors by the pitching-poor Pittsburgh Pirates, Necciai had a 1–6 record with a 7.08 earned run average in 1952. A sore arm and ulcer ended the Rocket's career before it ever really started.

4. HECTOR ESPINO

Hector Espino was the Babe Ruth of the minors. In a career that lasted from 1960 to 1984, he hit a minor league record 484 home runs. Espino spent most of his career in the Mexican Leagues because he claimed he was offended by the racial discrimination he had witnessed while playing for Jacksonville of the International League in 1964. Although the Cardinals, Mets, and Padres were interested in signing him, Espino turned down their offers because he did not want to play in the United States.

5. WALTER MALMQUIST

In 1913, Walter Malmquist set a professional baseball record when he batted .477 for York in the Nebraska State League. Despite his minor league heroics, Malmquist never reached the majors.

6. BOB RIESENER

Bob Riesener must have wondered what a guy had to do to make the majors. In 1957, pitching for Alexandria of the Class C Evangeline League, Riesener had a perfect 20–0 record. Buried in the talent-rich New York Yankees organization, he never played in the major leagues.

7. NIG CLARKE

Without a doubt the greatest power display in a professional game was an eight-home-run outburst by catcher Nig Clarke. He led his Corsicana team to a 51–3 rout of Texarkana in a game played on June 15, 1902. Clarke hit only six home runs in nine major league seasons.

8. BILL THOMAS

Bill Thomas pitched in more than 1,000 minor league games between 1926 and 1952. His 383 wins is a minor league record. Despite his success, Thomas toiled his entire career in the minors.

9. BOB CRUES

In 1948, Bob Crues hit sixty-nine home runs (including eight grand slams) and batted .404 for Amarillo of the West Texas-New Mexico League. His 254 runs batted in was a professional single season record. Like so many minor league record breakers, Crues never played in the major leagues.

10. TOM LASORDA

Lefthander Tom Lasorda struck out twenty-five batters while pitching for the Schnectady Blue Jays against the Amsterdam Rugmakers in 1948. In three major league seasons, two in Dodger blue, Lasorda had a 0–4 record and a 6.48 earned run average.

False Promise

It's always exciting when a young player breaks into the majors with a bang. More often than not, these players fail to live up to our expectations. Brooklyn outfielder Jack Dalton got five hits off Christy Mathewson in his second game but hit only .213 against the rest of the league. Frank Ernaga of the Chicago Cubs hit a home run and triple off Warren Spahn in his first two at-bats and had five extra base hits in his first eight at-bats. After the hot start, Ernaga had only two more extra base hits in the majors. All of the following players' best moments came at the very beginning of their careers.

1. BOBO HOLLOMAN

On May 6, 1953, Bobo Holloman of the St. Louis Browns pitched a no-hitter versus Philadelphia in his first major league start. The evening was so cold and rainy that owner Bill Veeck announced before the start of the game that rain checks would be provided for the 2,473 fans in attendance. Veeck was so impressed with the outing that he exercised a $25,000 option on the pitcher, instead of using the money to purchase the contract of minor league shortstop Ernie Banks. Holloman won only two more games in the majors while Banks had a Hall of Fame career in Chicago.

2. KARL SPOONER

In his major league debut on September 22, 1954, Brooklyn southpaw Karl Spooner struck out fifteen as he pitched a three-hit shutout against the pennant-winning New York Giants. Four days later, he fanned twelve in a four-hit whitewash of Pittsburgh. Spooner injured his arm the next spring and won only eight games. He was given the chance to start game six of the 1955 World Series against the New York Yankees. If he won, it would finally have ended the domination the Yanks had over the Dodgers in the fall classic. Spooner was shelled for five runs in the first inning, which proved to be his final appearance in the major leagues. The next day, another young lefthander, Johnny Podres, became a hero by shutting out the Yankees. Spooner's spot on the roster was filled by another promising southpaw. His name was Sandy Koufax.

3. CLINT HARTUNG

Perhaps the biggest bust in baseball history was Clint Hartung. Ballyhooed as the next Babe Ruth, Hartung had batted .567 and was 25–0 as a pitcher while playing for armed services teams during World War II. He showed promise as a rookie, batting .309 and compiling a 9–7 record as a pitcher with New York in 1947. The Giants couldn't decide if he should be a pitcher or play in the outfield. Soon it became apparent that he was a double threat: he couldn't pitch and he couldn't hit. On the mound his career earned run average was a dismal 5.02, and his batting average dipped to .238. Originally known as the "Hondo Hurricane," Hartung was later referred to as "Floppy."

4. BILL ROHR

In his major league debut on April 14, 1969, Boston lefthander Bob Rohr pitched eight innings of no-hit ball before New York's Elston Howard broke it up with a single. Rohr won only two more games and was through by the time he was twenty-two.

5. PAUL PETTIT

Paul Pettit was considered a can't-miss prospect. Pettit had pitched six no-hitters in high school and was brought to the majors at the age of nineteen by Pittsburgh in 1951. In his contract, the club promised to pay for an all-expenses paid honeymoon in Hawaii if he got married and called for a movie deal to film his life story if he became a star. The cameras never started rolling as Pettit won only one game in the major leagues.

6. JOE PATE

Joe Pate was 9–0 as a rookie pitcher with the Philadelphia A's in 1926. After the auspicious start, Pate never won another game in the major leagues.

7. RUSS VAN ATTA

Russ Van Atta may have had the greatest debut in major league history. On April 25, 1933, the Yankees' southpaw pitched a shutout against Washington, winning the game 16–0. He also had four hits in the game. After a 12–4 rookie season, Van Atta compiled a 21–37 record with a 5.60 career earned run average.

8. LEFTY RUSSELL

Philadelphia's Lefty Russell pitched a shutout in his major league debut on October 1, 1910. He lost his remaining five decisions in the majors, and his earned run average soared to 6.36.

9. **BILL ROMAN**

Detroit first baseman Bill Roman hit a home run in his first major league at-bat on September 30, 1964. Roman had only four more hits in the major leagues, and his lifetime batting average was an anemic .143.

10. **JESSE STOVALL**

Cleveland lefthander Jesse Stovall pitched an eleven-inning shutout in his major league debut on September 3, 1903. Stovall was out of baseball after a 3–13 record the next season.

One Game Wonders

One of the wonderful things about baseball is that anyone can become a hero for a day. These players had undistinguished careers interrupted by a game of a lifetime.

1. JOHN PACIOREK

John Paciorek was eighteen years old when he played his first game with the Houston Astros on September 29, 1963. He went three for three, walked twice, scored four runs, and batted in three. You could say he played the game of his life. You can say that because it was his only major league game. The next season Paciorek injured his back and batted only .135 in the minor leagues.

2. TOM CHENEY

Tom Cheney did something that Roger Clemens, Randy Johnson, Nolan Ryan, Steve Carlton, Tom

Seaver, and Sandy Koufax were never able to do. On September 12, 1962, Cheney, pitching for the Washington Senators, struck out twenty-one batters in a sixteen-inning game against Baltimore. The twenty-one strikeouts is a major league record for a pitcher in a single game. The record for a nine-inning game is twenty, shared by Roger Clemens and Kerry Wood. Cheney never had a winning season and finished his eight-year career with a 19–29 record.

3. CHARLIE ROBERTSON

In only his third major league game, Chicago White Sox pitcher Charlie Robertson pitched a perfect game against the Detroit Tigers on April 30, 1922. His stuff was so outstanding that Tiger players Ty Cobb and Harry Heilmann complained throughout the game that Robertson was doctoring the ball. In the ninth inning the umpire went to the mound and examined his uniform and glove but found no foreign substances. Robertson never recreated the magic of that day and had a dreadful 49–80 lifetime record.

4. CESAR GUTIERREZ

Light-hitting Detroit Tigers shortstop Cesar Gutierrez went seven for seven in a game on June 21, 1970. He tied the major league record for the most hits in a game without making an out. The seven hits matched his total for the entire 1971 season, his last in the majors.

5. RAY JANSEN

St. Louis Browns' third baseman Ray Jansen collected four hits in five at-bats in his big league debut on September 30, 1910. He never played another game, closing out his career with a .800 batting average.

6. MARK WHITEN

For most of his career, Mark Whiten has been a journeyman player, but on September 7, 1993, he tied two of baseball's most impressive single game records. The St. Louis outfielder hit four home runs and batted in twelve runs in the second game of a doubleheader against Cincinnati. Whiten is the only player to have both four homers and twelve RBIs in the same game. His final homer was a 440-foot shot to center field off Reds' flamethrowing reliever, Rob Dibble.

7. FLOYD GIEBELL

In the final days of the 1940 season, Detroit and Cleveland were locked in a close pennant race. On September 27 the Indians were scheduled to pitch their ace, Bob Feller. Unexpectedly, Detroit manager Del Baker handed the ball to rookie Floyd Giebell. The rookie shocked everyone by defeating Feller and the Indians 2–0 to clinch the pennant for Detroit. For Giebell, it was the third victory of his career, and his last.

8. KEN ASH

Ken Ash could be classified as a one-inning wonder. On July 27, 1930, the Cincinnati Reds reliever entered the game against Chicago in the sixth inning. With no outs and runners on first and second, Ash enticed Charlie Grimm to hit into a triple play on his first pitch. Ash had recorded three outs on just one pitch. The Reds rallied to win 6–5, and Ash was the winner, one of only six victories he was credited with in the majors.

9. GENE STEPHENS

Another one-inning wonder was Boston outfielder Gene Stephens. The Red Sox set an American League record when they scored seventeen runs in the seventh inning of a game against Detroit on June 11, 1953. Stephens set another record when he became the only modern player to collect three hits in an inning. Catcher Sammy White also set a record when he scored three runs. Groomed to be the replacement for Red Sox legend Ted Williams, Stephens never played regularly in the majors in twelve seasons.

10. PHIL WEINTRAUB

First baseman Phil Weintraub had played for the Giants, Reds, and Phillies between 1933 and 1938. After being out of the majors for six years, Weintraub was given another chance to play because many major leaguers were in the military during World War II. Weintraub made the most of his comeback with a career day on April 30, 1944. He batted in eleven runs, one short of the record, in a 26–8 Giants victory over Brooklyn. In seven major league seasons, Weintraub averaged fewer than thirty RBIs per season.

One Year Wonders

Superstars are players who are great every year. Some players only achieve greatness for one season. They are baseball's one-year wonders.

Zoilo "Zorro" Versalles
Minnesota shortstop Zoilo Versalles was the American League Most Valuable Player in 1965, a performance he never came close to duplicating.

1. ROSS BARNES

The National League's first star was Chicago second baseman Ross Barnes. He hit the first home run in National League history on May 2, 1876. That year he led the league in hits, runs, doubles, bases on balls, batting average, and slugging percentage. His .429 batting average was the result of his mastery of the fair-foul rule. Under the rules of the day, if any ball hit fair and kicked foul, it was in play. Barnes perfected the art of slapping balls that skipped foul and were almost impossible to defense. When the rule was changed the following season, his batting average plummeted 157 points. When Barnes missed some games due to a muscle injury, owner William Hulbert withheld $1,000 of his $2,500 salary.

2. FRED DUNLAP

The Union Association lasted only one year—1884. The unquestioned star of the league was second baseman Fred "Sureshot" Dunlap. Dunlap had signed with the new league for a record $3,400 per year. He led the Union Association in batting, hits, home runs, runs scored, and slugging percentage. When he returned to the National League in 1885, Dunlap's average dropped from .412 to .270.

3. JOCKO FLYNN

Jocko Flynn was the ultimate one-year wonder. In 1886, Flynn was 24–6 and led the National League in winning percentage while pitching for Chicago. For unknown reasons, he never pitched another game in the major leagues.

4. NED WILLIAMSON

Ned Williamson was light-hitting third baseman during the early years of the National League. Known primarily for his defensive skills, he became a slugger when the fences of Chicago's Lake Front Park were moved in to 196 feet in right field and 180 feet in left. Thanks to the short fences, Williamson hit a record twenty-seven home runs in 1884. He had never hit more than three in any of his first six seasons. When the fences were moved back the next year, Williamson's homer total fell to three. His record stood for thirty-five years until Babe Ruth hit twenty-nine in 1919.

5. EARL WEBB

In 1931, Boston outfielder Earl Webb set a single season record for doubles that still stands. His sixty-seven doubles were thirty-seven more than he had in any other season.

6. GEORGE WATKINS

Cardinals' outfielder George Watkins batted a sensational .373 in 119 games during his rookie season in 1930. After his fantastic rookie year, Watkins's average fell eighty-five points the next season.

7. ZOILO VERSALLES

Versalles was the runaway Most Valuable Player winner in 1965. The Twins' shortstop led the American League in at-bats, doubles, triples, and runs. His leadership helped Minnesota win their first pennant. Bothered by back problems, he never hit above .250 again.

8. BOB HAZLE

Brought up from the minors in July 1957, Bob "Hurricane" Hazle tore up the National League and was a major reason why the Milwaukee Braves won their first pennant. The next year Hurricane's average dipped from .403 to .179, and he was shipped to Detroit.

9. BILLY TAYLOR

In 1884 pitcher Billy Taylor won forty-three games while dividing his season between St. Louis of the Union Association and Philadelphia of the American Association. He won only seven games in six other seasons.

10. FRANK KNAUSS

As a rookie pitcher with Columbus of the American Association in 1890, Frank Knauss won seventeen games. He played four more seasons in the major leagues, but never won another game.

Going Batty

B ats can be the hitter's best friend and the pitcher's worst nightmare. Sluggers Josh Gibson and Darryl Strawberry were known to kiss their bats. Frankie Frisch hung bats in his barn to "cure" them. It was rumored that Joe Sewell, the hardest man in baseball history to strike out, used the same bat throughout his fourteen-year career. Ripper Collins collected broken bats that he used to build fences on his estate in Rochester, New York. Take a few swings with these sluggers.

1. PETE "THE GLADIATOR" BROWNING

One of the great students of hitting, Pete "The Gladiator" Browning is the man responsible for starting the customized bat industry. In 1884, Browning walked into the J. F. Hillerich's wood shop in his hometown of Louisville, Kentucky.

Browning was in a rare slump and ordered a bat made to his exact specifications. He immediately broke out of the slump and extolled the virtues of his personalized bat throughout the league. Overnight the small wood shop became Hillerich & Bradsby, the world's largest bat manufacturer and maker of the famed Louisville Slugger. Browning owned more than 700 bats, each of which he gave a name, often biblical in origin. The Gladiator won three batting titles and had a .343 lifetime batting average.

2. HACK MILLER

Hack Miller was the strong man of baseball. He performed amazing feats of strength, such as bending iron bars and pounding spikes into wood with his fist. Miller generally used a forty-seven-ounce bat, but once toted a sixty-five-ouncer to the plate. Between 1916 and 1925, the outfielder compiled a .323 lifetime batting average.

3. BILL "LITTLE EVA" LANGE

Bill "Little Eva" Lange was one of the best and most popular players of the 1890s. A great showman, Lange once went to the plate with a bat nearly six feet long, almost two-and-one-half feet longer than regulation. Little Eva hit a grounder and reached base on an error.

4. **EDDIE GAEDEL**

Only three feet seven inches tall, Eddie Gaedel was the smallest player ever to appear in a major league game. Sent up to pinch hit for the St. Louis Browns in a game against Detroit on August 19, 1951, Gaedel came to the plate carrying a toylike 17-inch bat, less than half the size of a normal bat. Instructed by owner Bill Veeck not to swing, Gaedel crouched at the plate, making it virtually impossible for Detroit pitcher Bob Cain to throw a strike. Gaedel was walked on four pitches.

5. **TY COBB**

Ty Cobb's .366 lifetime batting average is easily the best in baseball history. Cobb named his forty-two-ounce black bat "Magic." No one was permitted to touch it, and Cobb rarely let it out of his sight. The Georgia Peach once brought his bat to a wedding and frequently dined with it.

6. **HEINIE GROH**

Third baseman Heinie Groh played for the 1919 world champion Cincinnati Reds and was a mainstay with the New York Giants' championship teams of the early 1920s. Groh's trademark was his bottle bat, a specially designed bat with a thick barrel and tapered handle. Using his bottle bat, Groh twice led the league in doubles.

7. RICHIE ASHBURN

Hall of Fame outfielder Richie Ashburn was one of the game's great contact hitters. A .308 lifetime hitter, Ashburn was the National League batting champion in 1955 and 1958. Once, when Ashburn was mired in a rare slump, he took his bat to bed. "I wanted to know my bat a little better," he reasoned.

8. WEE WILLIE KEELER

Wee Willie Keeler stood only five feet four inches tall and used the smallest bat (with the exception of Eddie Gaedel) in professional baseball history. The bat was thirty inches long and only 2.5 inches in diameter. Keeler choked up halfway on the bat and mastered the Baltimore Chop in which he would hit down on the ball, allowing him to beat out infield hits. His .345 career batting average is fifth all-time, and his .432 average in 1897 is the best ever for a lefthanded batter.

9. JOHNNY MIZE

Slugger Johnny Mize used sixty bats, each one for a different pitcher. He used longer bats for lefthanders so he could reach pitches tailing away from him. Mize practiced his swing in the hotel room while puffing on a cigar. The "Big Cat" led the National League in home runs in 1939, 1940, 1947, and 1948.

10. EDDIE COLLINS

Eddie Collins played in the major leagues between 1906 and 1933 and was one of the greatest second basemen in baseball history. Collins sometimes buried his bats in shallow holes he called "graves" to "keep them lively." It must have worked because Collins wrapped out 3,311 hits in his long career.

Having a Ball

Baseballs used in major league games are uniform in size and weight. Each one weighs 5 to 5¼ ounces, measures 9 to 9¼ inches in circumference, and is 3 inches in diameter. The liveliness of the ball seems to vary from year to year. There have been dead ball eras as well as periods when juiced balls were in play. As evidenced by this chapter, some unusual things can be done to the horsehide during a game.

1. WILLIAM "BLONDIE" PURCELL

In the early days of baseball, umpires rarely removed a ball from play no matter how dirty or scuffed it was. On June 6, 1882, Buffalo pitcher Pud Galvin was having trouble throwing a curve because the ball was so soggy. Teammate Blondie Purcell cut the baseball in half so that the umpire would be forced to give Galvin a new one.

2. ED WALSH

Ed Walsh fashioned a 1.82 career earned run average, the lowest in the history of baseball. His secret to success was the nastiest spitter in the game. During Walsh's career, from 1904 to 1917, the spitball was a legal pitch. Sam Crawford complained that Walsh's wet one was so loaded up that all he could see was spit going by. Walsh licked the ball rather than spitting on it. The Philadelphia A's tried to break him of the unsanitary habit by rubbing horse manure on the horsehide. "I vomited all over the place," Walsh admitted. He retaliated by throwing beanballs at all the A's hitters.

3. WHITEY FORD

The New York Yankees won eleven pennants while Whitey Ford was their ace. The "Chairman of the Board" won 236 games and his .690 winning percentage is the third best in baseball history. Ford doctored the ball in more ways than any other pitcher. He cut the ball with a ring or sometimes had catcher Elston Howard slice it with a buckle on his shin guard. He perfected the "mud ball," which he loaded up while reaching for the resin bag. Ford's greatest creation was the "gunk" ball. The magic formula consisted of baby oil, turpentine, and resin. Whitey kept the concoction in a roll-on deodorant bottle. Unsuspecting,

Whitey Ford
Throwing illegal pitches such as the mud ball and gunk ball, Yankees' ace Whitey Ford won 236 games.

teammate Yogi Berra once used the deodorant after a shower and ran screaming from the locker room with his arms glued to his sides.

4. RUSS FORD

Not as well known as Whitey, Russ Ford nevertheless won twenty games three times between 1910 and 1914. Ford was the man credited with the discovery that if a pitcher scuffed the ball, it would dip in a manner that would make it extremely difficult to hit. He developed the emery ball, which he would scuff with emery paper concealed in his glove.

5. **SMOKEY JOE WILLIAMS**

Smokey Joe Williams pitched from 1905 to 1932 and was one of the greatest stars of the Negro Leagues. He once struck out twenty while no-hitting the New York Giants in 1917, and fanned twenty-seven in a Negro League game. Besides his blazing fastball, Smokey Joe had an arsenal of illegal pitches: sandpapered ball, emery ball, and his specialty, the goo ball on which he rubbed a black, tarlike substance.

6. **RICK HONEYCUTT**

Rick Honeycutt had a long and successful career as a pitcher, highlighted by an earned run average title in 1983. The low point of his career was in 1980 when he was discovered cutting a ball with a tack he had taped to his finger. Absent-mindedly, he rubbed his finger across his face, cutting himself and narrowly missing taking his eye out.

7. **BOBBY MATHEWS**

The dubious distinction of being the inventor of the spitball belongs to Bobby Mathews. He won thirty games three consecutive seasons for Philadelphia from 1883 to 1885. Mathews was the first to realize that moisture placed on the ball causes it to drop dramatically just as it reaches the plate. Since the ball was blackened in those days, Mathews used the saliva to create a white spot, about the size of a quarter. The optical illusion also contributed to the effectiveness of the pitch.

8. HOD ELLER

Hod Eller was a twenty-game winner for the champion 1919 Cincinnati Reds and won two games during the World Series against the Chicago White Sox. Eller was the creator of the shineball, an erratically moving pitch that resulted from rubbing talcum powder on the baseball.

9. LARRY MACPHAIL

Larry MacPhail was the visionary executive who introduced night baseball. One of his innovations that failed, though, was yellow baseballs. Mac-Phail believed that the colored baseballs would be easier to see. They were used in four games during the 1938 season but were never adopted by the major leagues.

10. CHARLIE FINLEY

Oakland A's owner Charlie Finley, the man who brought the game white shoes and green and gold uniforms, tried to introduce orange baseballs to the national pastime. In 1973, he experimented with the orange-colored balls during spring training. Finley argued that the orange balls reduced the glare of the lights during night games. Like MacPhail's yellow balls, orange baseballs never gained acceptance.

Records that Aren't Meant to Be Broken

Records are meant to be broken. They said that Babe Ruth's career home run mark would never be broken, until Hank Aaron passed him in 1974. Ty Cobb's 4,191 career base hits seemed unassailable until Pete Rose came along. Joe Di-Maggio's fifty-six-game hitting streak is often cited as the current record least likely to be broken. Here are some records even more unapproachable.

1. **JACK TAYLOR**

Perhaps the record least likely to be broken is Jack Taylor's mark of 188 consecutive complete games. Today's pitchers rarely finish what they start. From June 20, 1901 until August 9, 1906, Taylor was never knocked out of the box. His 1.33 earned run average in 1902 led the National League.

2. **WILL WHITE**

Almost totally forgotten today, pitcher Will White three times won forty or more games in a season. He set two single season records in 1879 while pitching for Cincinnati that will never be broken. White pitched seventy-five complete games and hurled 680 innings.

3. **CY YOUNG**

The great Cy Young won 511 games during his illustrious career that lasted from 1890 to 1911. To put the record in perspective, a player could win 20 games for twenty-five consecutive seasons and still fall 11 victories short.

4. **OLD HOSS RADBOURNE**

Today, twenty wins in a season is the standard of excellence for a pitcher. In 1884, Old Hoss Radbourne won sixty games pitching for Providence, a record that will almost certainly never be broken. Proving that figure was no fluke, he won forty-nine games the following season.

5. **WAHOO SAM CRAWFORD**

Hall of Fame outfielder Sam Crawford's career mark of 312 triples will never be challenged. He led the league in triples six times between 1902 and 1915. Crawford had the perfect combination of speed and power and played in the dead ball era when home runs were scarce.

6. OWEN WILSON

Another triple threat was Pittsburgh outfielder Owen Wilson. In 1912, he legged out thirty-six three baggers, a record not likely to be surpassed. Wilson never had more than fourteen triples in any other season.

7. MATCHES KILROY

When Nolan Ryan struck out 383 batters in 1973, he set the modern single season strikeout record. The Express still fell 130 strikeouts short of the record established by Matches Kilroy, who struck out 513 during his rookie season with Baltimore in 1886. Although Kilroy led the American Association with forty-six wins the next year, he never struck out more than 217 in a season for the remainder of his career.

8. HUGH DUFFY

It's been more than fifty years since Ted Williams was the last player to hit .400 in a season. Boston outfielder Hugh Duffy's record average of .438, which he achieved in the 1894 season, seems safe for at least another half-century.

9. BILLY HAMILTON

Sliding Billy Hamilton was one of the best players of the nineteenth century. In 1894, while playing with Philadelphia, he scored a record 196 runs. To put the achievement in perspective, when Ricky Henderson scored 146 runs in 1985 (the most in the majors since 1948), he still fell 50 runs short of Hamilton's record.

10. CLYDE BARNHART

Pittsburgh rookie third sacker Clyde Barnhart became the only major leaguer to hit safely in three games in one day. It occurred on October 2, 1920 in a rare tripleheader against Cincinnati.

The Mendoza Line

Bob Uecker has made a career joking about his poor hitting. Uecker's .200 career batting average undoubtedly gave him a lot of material. Mario Mendoza was a weak-hitting shortstop who played between 1974 and 1982. George Brett claimed that he always looked at the weekly listing of batting averages to see who was below the "Mendoza Line." The Mendoza Line has come to signify anyone hitting less than .200. Mendoza, a lifetime .215 hitter (who became a hitting instructor after he retired as a player), was Ty Cobb compared to the men included in this section.

1. BILL BERGEN

As a poor hitter, catcher Bill Bergen was in a class of his own. His .170 career batting average is 42 points lower than any other player with at least

2,500 at-bats. His .139 average in 1909 (he had only three extra base hits in 346 at-bats) is the lowest ever for a player with enough plate appearances to qualify for a batting title. Bergen finished 200 points behind batting champion Honus Wagner that season.

2. RON HERBEL

If Bill Bergen was the worst hitting nonpitcher, Ron Herbel may have been the worst hitter of all time. Herbel finished his major league career in 1971 with an all-time low .029 batting average, collecting only six hits in 206 at-bats. Only once in nine seasons did he have more than one hit.

3. BOB BUHL

Bob Buhl was a pretty good pitcher (166–132 lifetime record) who was a really bad hitter (.089 career batting average). In 1962, he set the standard for futility by going hitless in seventy at-bats.

4. JOHN VUKOVICH

John Vukovich was a utility player during the 1970s who was a futility player at the plate. Vukovich played all the infield positions and couldn't hit at any of them. In ten seasons, he compiled a horrible .161 batting average, averaging only nine hits per season.

5. **RAY OYLER**

Ray Oyler was such a bad hitter that the fans in Seattle formed a fan club. Members marveled at his sheer ineptitude with the bat. A .175 lifetime hitter, Oyler was replaced at shortstop by outfielder Mickey Stanley in the 1968 World Series after hitting a career low of .135 in 215 at-bats in 1968.

6. **BILL HOLBERT**

When catcher Bill Holbert came to the plate, there was an instant power outage. Over his twelve-year major league career, from 1876 to 1888, Holbert had 2,335 at-bats and never hit a home run. His career batting average was a dismal .208.

7. **TOMMY THEVENOW**

Shortstop Tommy Thevenow hit the only two regular season home runs of his career in 1926. For the next twelve seasons, Thevenow came to the plate a record 3,347 times without a homer.

8. **DAL MAXVILL**

Dal Maxvill personified the old adage "good field, no hit." In 1970, the Cardinals' shortstop set the record for the fewest number of hits (80) and fewest extra base hits (7) for a player appearing in 150 games. He proved it was no fluke by collecting only 80 hits again the following season.

9. BURLEIGH GRIMES

Burleigh Grimes was a Hall of Fame pitcher (270 wins) and a decent hitter (.248 batting average). However, in a 1925 game, he accounted for seven outs in only three at-bats. In consecutive at-bats "Ol' Stubblebeard" hit into two double plays and a triple play.

10. BUDDY BIACALANA

Kansas City infielder Buddy Biacalana's hitting (or lack of it) was the butt of jokes made by David Letterman on his *Late Night* show. He kept a nightly countdown of how many hits Biacalana needed to pass Pete Rose as the all-time hit leader. Biacalana finished with 113, only 4,143 short of Rose. Not appreciating the comparisons, Buddy remarked, "I'm still a lot closer to Rose than he is in pursuit of Johnny Carson."

Sultans of Swish

J oe Sewell was the hardest man in major league
history to strike out, fanning only once every
62.6 at-bats. By contrast, Dave Nicholson headed
back to the dugout every 2.4 at-bats. The chapter is dedicated to the Kings of the K.

1. REGGIE JACKSON

The undisputed strikeout champion has to be
Reggie Jackson. He fanned 2,597 times, 661
times more than his closest rival, Willie Stargell.
Eighteen seasons Reggie whiffed more than 100
times, peaking at 171 in 1968. In essence, Jackson struck out the equivalent of four full seasons.

2. DAVE NICHOLSON

1940s slugger Bill Nicholson earned the nickname "Swish" because of his classic strikeout
form. The nickname really should have belonged

to Dave Nicholson, the 1960s outfielder who took the art of striking out to a new level. Dave struck out once every 2.48 at-bats, a record. His banner year was 1963 when he struck out what was then a record 175 times. He tied another record by fanning four times in a game on three separate occasions.

3. BOBBY BONDS

Bobby Bonds was not your typical leadoff hitter. He hit 332 home runs and struck out 1,757 times. In 1969, he set a major league record by striking out 187 times. The next season he upped the mark to 189. Ten times he fanned 120 or more times in a season.

4. JIMMIE FOXX

Ninety-seven of baseball's top one hundred career strikeout kings have played in the second half of the twentieth century. The only two old-timers to rank in the top fifty are Babe Ruth and Jimmie Foxx. "Double X" set a record by leading the American League in strikeouts seven times.

5. PETE INCAVIGLIA

Pete Incaviglia was the NCAA Player of the Year at Oklahoma State in 1985. In 1986, the rookie

Rangers' outfielder set an American League record with 185 strikeouts. He fanned 168 times the next season, thus proving it was no fluke.

6. ROB DEER

During his career from 1984 to 1993, outfielder Rob Deer struck out 1,379 times in only 3,831 at-bats. Deer fanned 186 times in 1987 and 179 the previous year.

7. GORMAN THOMAS

Milwaukee outfielder Gorman Thomas struck out 1,339 times in 4,677 at-bats. He led the American League with 175 strikeouts in 1979 and 170 the following season.

8. WOODIE HELD

An underappreciated strikeout artist, Woodie Held struck out nearly once every four times during his fourteen-year career, which ended in 1969. What made Woodie stand out were the frequent tantrums that followed his strikeouts.

9. WILLIE STARGELL

Willie Stargell is the all-time National League strikeout leader with 1,936. He struck out 100 or more times twelve consecutive years and led the league with 154 in 1971.

10. **VINCE DIMAGGIO**

The older brother of Joe DiMaggio, Vince led the National League in strikeouts a record six times. His 134 whiffs during the 1938 season set a record since eclipsed.

The Worst Pitching Performances of All Time

B atting practice usually occurs before the game, but in these instances the batters took batting practice after the National Anthem was sung. Here are the creme de la creme of badly pitched games.

1. JACK WADSWORTH

Perhaps the worst pitcher of all time, Jack Wadsworth also pitched the worst game in major league history. On August 17, 1894, Wadsworth, pitching for the Louisville Colonels, was mauled for twenty-nine runs and thirty-six hits by Philadelphia. Sam Thompson had six hits and hit for the cycle while three other teammates had five hits each. For his career, Wadsworth fashioned a 6–38 record with a 6.58 earned run average.

2. C. B. DEWITT

On June 15, 1902, the Corsicana Oilers walloped the Texarkana Tigers 51–3 in a Texas League game. Pitcher C. B. DeWitt (who also owned the team) was shellacked for fifty-one runs and fifty-three hits. He surrendered twenty-one home runs, eight of them to Nig Clarke.

3. DAVE ROWE

Cleveland outfielder Dave Rowe was asked to pitch a game against Chicago on July 24, 1882. Rowe was roughed up for twenty-nine hits and thirty-five runs in a 35–4 drubbing. Rowe pitched four games during his career, giving up fifty-four hits in twenty-three innings and compiling a 9.78 earned run average.

4. AL TRAVERS

In May 1912, Ty Cobb was suspended after beating a heckler senseless. His Tiger teammates went on strike to support Cobb. On May 18, Detroit faced the mighty Philadelphia Athletics with a team composed of amateurs and coaches. Seminary student Al Travers pitched a complete game, giving up twenty-four runs and twenty-six hits in a 24–2 loss. Cobb was soon reinstated, and Travers never pitched in another major league game.

5. DOC PARKER

Righthander Doc Parker gave up twenty-one runs and twenty-six hits against Brooklyn in his first game with Cincinnati in 1901. Batters were so eager to face Parker that they ran to the plate. "The next time I get in the box I hope to give a better account of myself," Parker vowed. For Parker, though, there would be no next time.

6. **ED ROMMEL**

Philadelphia A's owner Connie Mack decided to send only two pitchers on a one-day road trip to Cleveland. When starter Lew Krausse was knocked out in the first inning, reliever Ed Rommel entered the game. The game lasted eighteen innings with the A's prevailing 18–17. Rommel gave up twenty-nine hits, a record for a reliever, but still got the win. Cleveland's Johnny Burnett had a record nine hits in the game.

7. **STUMP WEIDMAN**

Stump Weidman led the National League in earned run average (1.80) in 1881. For most of his career, Stump was less successful. On September 6, 1883, Weidman gave up a record thirteen base hits in an inning while pitching for Detroit. In 1886, he led the National League in losses, with thirty-six.

8. **WILLIAM REIDY**

In 1901, Milwaukee pitcher William Reidy gave up a record ten consecutive hits in the ninth inning of a 13–2 loss to Boston. Reidy was a twenty-game loser that season.

9. JOE CLEARY

Making his major league debut on August 4, 1945, Joe Cleary of the Washington Senators was tagged for seven runs in one-third of an inning by the Boston Red Sox. His 189.00 career earned run average is the worst in major league history.

10. BIFF WYSONG

On August 10, 1930, lefthander Biff Wysong made his major league debut against Philadelphia. Wysong was honored in a special Appreciation Day by residents of his hometown, Clarksville, Ohio. Biff was knocked out of the box in the third inning as the Phillies routed the Reds 18–0. The Reds didn't appreciate Wysong's 19.29 earned run average and shipped him to the minors.

I'm a Loser

Some people just can't win. Although he had a respectable 3.62 earned run average, Steve Gerken went 0–12 with a Philadelphia A's club that won only fifty-two games in 1945. Happy Jack Townsend's 35–82 lifetime record left him with little to smile about. Dory Dean (4–26 career record) was never confused with Dizzy Dean. Other pitchers with a L next to their name in the box score were Buster Brown (48–105), Ike Pearson (13–50), Bill Bailey (34–78), and Kirtley Baker (9–38). If you think it can't get any worse than that, then read on.

1. TERRY FELTON

Terry Felton deserves special recognition as the pitcher who lost the most games without ever winning one. In 1980, he previewed things to come by going 0–3 with a 7.00 earned run average for the Minnesota Twins. The next season he made his one appearance memorable by giving up six runs in one inning. Felton ended his career with a flourish in 1982, losing all thirteen decisions. For his career Felton was a perfect 0–16.

2. ANTHONY YOUNG

Terry Felton would have had to lose a dozen more games to break the record of Anthony Young. From May 6, 1991 until July 24, 1993, Young lost an incredible twenty-seven straight decisions.

3. CLIFF CURTIS

On June 13, 1910, Boston righthander Cliff Curtis began a streak of twenty-three consecutive losses. A victim of nonsupport, Curtis had a career record of 28–61 in spite of a decent 3.31 earned run average.

4. JACK NABORS

Jack Nabors' career record of 1–25 is partly attributable to the fact that he played for the horrendous Philadelphia Athletics teams of 1915 and 1916. After a five-year championship run (1910–14), owner Connie Mack sold off his best players. Nabors was 0–5 as a rookie. Then he lost nineteen in a row during a 1–20 season for the 1916 A's (36–117), the worst record of any team of the twentieth century. Nabors was only the third losingest pitcher on the team.

5. JOHN COLEMAN

During his rookie season in 1883, Philadelphia pitcher John Coleman set records that will never be broken. Coleman lost forty-eight games and gave up 772 hits. Wisely, he played most of the rest of his career in the outfield. Coleman closed out his career in 1890 with twenty-three wins and seventy-two losses.

6. JOE HARRIS

Joe Harris was not the luckiest pitcher ever to play the game. Pitching for Boston between 1905 and 1907, Harris won three and lost thirty. In 1906, he led the American League in losses with twenty-one, including fourteen in a row. Even when he pitched a good game, he lost. He set an American League record by dueling with Philadelphia's Jack Coombs for twenty-four innings. Naturally, Harris lost, 4–1.

7. HUGH MULCAHY

Philadelphia's Hugh Mulcahy earned the nickname "Losing Pitcher" by leading the National League in losses in both 1938 and 1940. Phillies' fans thought their luck might be changing when

Mulcahy was the first major leaguer inducted into the service during World War II. How he fared during the war is a mystery, although Philadelphia fans may have suspected that any grenades he threw were probably lined back through his legs. Mulcahy did fight on the winning side in the war. Unfortunately, he was 45–89 lifetime, the worst winning percentage in the twentieth century for a hurler with more than 100 decisions.

8. COLDWATER JIM HUGHEY

Coldwater Jim Hughey was the ace of the remarkable 1899 Cleveland Spiders' pitching staff. The Spiders had the worst record in baseball history (20–134), and they owed much of it to Hughey, who was 4–30 and led the National League in losses. Coldwater Jim (who received his nickname, surprisingly, not because of all the early showers he took but because his hometown was Coldwater, Michigan) was 29–80 during his seven years in the majors, and his winning percentage is the lowest for any pitcher with at least 100 decisions. Other pitchers in the Spiders' rotation included "Crazy" Schmidt (2–17), Frank (no relation to Norman) Bates (1–18), "Still" Bill Hill (3–6), and Harry Colliflower (1–11).

9. BOB GROOM

Bob Groom lost nineteen consecutive games during his rookie season with Washington in 1909. He led the league in losses in 1909, 1914, and 1917. On the plus side, Groom won twenty-four games in 1912 and pitched a no-hitter in 1917.

10. MARK LEMONGELLO

Mark Lemongello was 22–38 during his career, which lasted from 1976 to 1979. Probably nobody ever took a loss harder than Lemongello. When taken out of a game he was known to beat his pitching hand and once bit his shoulder until it bled. In his final major league start, he threw the ball at the head of manager Roy Hartsfield before stomping off to the clubhouse. Lemongello's most spectacular tantrum occurred when he threw himself onto the banquet table in the clubhouse and lay in the mayonnaise and mustard for an hour.

Gopher Balls

A surprising statistic is that nine of the top twelve pitchers who have served up the most career home runs are in the Hall of Fame, and the other three will be someday. Twilight Ed Killian went almost four seasons without giving up a home run and won 102 games in his career. Robin Roberts threw over 500 gopher balls and won nearly 300 games.

1. ROBIN ROBERTS

Robin Roberts gave up a record 505 round trippers during his nineteen-year career. Many of them were solo shots he gave up in games in which he had a comfortable lead. Since he led the National League in wins four seasons in a row (1952–55) and won twenty games in six consecutive seasons (1950–55), he can be forgiven.

2. **BERT BLYLEVEN**

Bert Blyleven won 287 games, one more than Robin Roberts. In 1986, he set the single season record when he surrendered 50 home runs. His 384 career gopher balls places him in the all-time top ten.

3. **FERGUSON JENKINS**

Ferguson Jenkins's total of 284 wins is almost identical to that of Robin Roberts. Like Roberts he won twenty games six seasons in a row from 1967 to 1972, with a perennial doormat (the Chicago Cubs). Fittingly, his 484 gopher balls rank him second only to Roberts.

4. **PHIL NIEKRO**

Phil Niekro's knuckler was usually so difficult to hit that he won 318 games between 1964 and 1987 and was elected to the Hall of Fame. Conversely, he gave up 482 home runs (third on the all-time list).

5. **PAUL FOYTACK**

Paul Foytack of the Los Angeles Angels entered the record books on July 31, 1963 when he gave up four consecutive home runs to the Cleveland Indians. The hitters were not exactly Murderers'

Row: Woodie Held, pitcher Pedro Ramos, Tito Francona, and Larry Brown. An embarrassed Foytack admitted that his control was so bad that the last home run came on a knockdown pitch.

6. PEDRO RAMOS

Ramos, who hit one of the consecutive home runs off Foytack, was no slouch himself in giving them up. He gave up 315 in his career, one every seven innings he pitched. His nadir occurred in 1957 when he was tagged for 43 homers.

7. JACK FISHER

Jack Fisher led the National League in losses in 1965 and 1967 while with the lowly Mets. He deserves inclusion here because he gave up two memorable homers. He was on the mound in 1960 when Ted Williams hit a dramatic home run in his final career at-bat. The next season Roger Maris hit his sixtieth home run off Fisher to tie Babe Ruth's record.

8. TRACY STALLARD

Tracy Stallard has become a footnote in baseball history because he was the pitcher who allowed Roger Maris's record-breaking sixty-first home run in 1961. Stallard tried to remove the stigma by correctly pointing out that Maris had hit sixty

Jack Fisher

Pitcher Jack Fisher gave up Ted Williams's final home run in 1960 and Roger Maris's record-tying 60th homer the following season.

others. He also had the misfortune of being the opposing pitcher when Jim Bunning pitched his perfect game in 1964.

9. **AL DOWNING**

Al Downing was a fine pitcher who led the American League in strikeouts in 1964 and won twenty games for the Dodgers in 1971. Despite his accomplishments, he will always be remembered as the man who gave up Hank Aaron's historic 715th home run on April 8, 1974.

10. **TOM ZACHARY**

Almost no one remembers that Guy Bush gave up Babe Ruth's 714th and final home run. Many fans know that Tom Zachary allowed Ruth's 60th in 1927. Zachary, not appreciative of his everlasting fame, commented, "If you really want to know the truth. I'd rather thrown at his big, fat head." Zachary and Ruth became teammates the next season when the pitcher was traded from the Senators to the Yankees. Zachary won a game in the 1928 World Series and had a perfect 12–0 record in 1929.

Wild Things

Sportswriter Dick Young once wrote of Brooklyn pitcher Rex Barney, "He'd have been a great pitcher if home plate were high and outside." Red Ames threw a record 156 wild pitches in his career. Let yourself lose all control and take a walk on the wild side.

1. BILL STEMMEYER

Cannonball Bill Stemmeyer was the original Wild Thing. In 1886, while playing for Boston, Cannonball threw sixty-four wild pitches in only forty-one games. Despite his control problems, he managed to win twenty-two games that season.

2. AMOS RUSIE

Amos Rusie, the Hoosier Cannonball, had more than 200 walks five consecutive seasons. Rusie set the all-time record with 289 free passes in 1890.

3. DICK WEIK

Dick Weik must have been wild from birth. He walked 15 batters in his first minor league game in 1946. Of his twenty-six major league starts, he walked 10 or more four times. In 213 innings, Weik walked 237 batters. He finished his wild ride in the majors in 1954 with a record of six wins and twenty-two losses.

4. BILL GEORGE

Twenty-two-year-old rookie New York pitcher Bill George set a record by walking sixteen batters in a game against Chicago on May 30, 1887. On three other occasions, George walked thirteen.

5. GEORGE VAN HALTREN

As a rookie with Chicago in 1887, George Van Haltren walked sixteen men in a game. An adequate pitcher (40–31 career record), Van Haltren made the transition to the outfield where he became a star. Despite having his career shortened by a broken leg, Van Haltren batted .316, had 2,532 hits, scored 1,539 runs, and stole 583 bases.

6. BRUNO HAAS

On June 23, 1915, Philadelphia A's pitcher Bruno Haas walked sixteen batters in a game against

New York. After walking twenty-eight in fourteen innings, Haas was released and never pitched in the major leagues again.

7. DOLLY GRAY

In 1909, Washington pitcher Dolly Gray walked eight batters in an inning, including seven in a row. By the time the Senators told Dolly goodbye, he had won only fifteen games and lost fifty-one.

8. RYNE DUREN

Pitcher Ryne Duren wore Coke-bottle-thick glasses to correct the 20/200 vision in his left eye. He intentionally threw his first warm-up pitch to the backstop to intimidate the hitter. In the minors, he once hit a batter in the on-deck circle. Columnist Jack Murray wrote that Duren was the first guy in history to pitch in Braille. In 1958, Duren, pitching for the Yankees, led the American League in saves with twenty. Wildness and excessive drinking, however, cut short a potentially great career. For his career Duren walked six batters for every nine innings.

9. TOMMY BYRNE

Tommy Byrne led the league in hit batsmen five times. From 1949 to 1951, he led the American League in walks. In 1951, Byrne walked 150 in

143 innings. During his career he walked 1,037 in 1,362 innings, nearly seven per game.

10. CHUCK STOBBS

Washington lefty Chuck Stobbs uncorked the wildest pitch on record. On May 20, 1956, facing Bob Kennedy of the Tigers, Stobbs heaved a pitch seventeen rows into the stands. Once the loser of fifteen consecutive games, Stobbs had a flare for the spectacular. He was the victim of what is considered by many to be the longest home run in history. On April 17, 1953, Mickey Mantle hit a blast off Stobbs that was measured at 565 feet.

Chuck Stobbs
Lefty Chuck Stobbs gave up a 565 foot home run to Mickey Mantle and once uncorked a wild pitch that landed in the 17th row of the grandstand.

Head Hunters

The secret weapon of the pitcher is the beanball. The tradition of awarding first base to a hit batsman began after former minister Will White plunked several players. Brooklyn pitcher Joe Black threw at seven consecutive Reds after being taunted from the bench. Jim Kern called a no-hitter any game that he didn't hit anyone. Meet the maestros of chin music.

1. STAN WILLIAMS

From the time Stan Williams entered major league baseball in 1958 until he retired in 1972, he was the most feared man in baseball. He kept a list of players whom he intended to hit. If a player homered off him, his name was placed in his book. Batters rating four stars were in trouble. Home run king Hank Aaron had five stars next to his name. After beaning Aaron on the helmet,

Williams apologized, "I meant to hit you in the neck." Williams kept a photo of Aaron in the locker room, at which he practiced throwing. If a batter made the mistake of digging in at the plate, Williams would walk off the mound and suggest that he dig the hole six feet deep.

2. DON DRYSDALE

Stan Williams's Dodgers teammate Don Drysdale was twice the pitcher he was and his equal as a headhunter. Drysdale led the National League five times and set a modern record with 154 hit batsmen. Ironically, his record fifty-eight consecutive scoreless innings (since broken by Orel Hershiser) was made possible because of a nullified hit batsman. It appeared the streak was over when Giants' catcher Dick Dietz was hit with the bases loaded. However, the umpire ruled Dietz did not make an effort to get out of the way of the pitch.

3. PHIL KNELL

In 1891, Columbus pitcher Phil Knell set a single season record when he hit fifty-four batters. Knell won twenty-eight games that year and led the American Association in shutouts.

4. SAL "THE BARBER" MAGLIE

Sal Maglie earned the nickname "The Barber" because of the close shaves he gave hitters.

Don Drysdale
Dodgers' pitcher Don Drysdale set a
modern record when he hit 154 batters
during his career.

Maglie admitted that he threw at batters' heads
because it was easier for them to move their
heads than their bodies. Pittsburgh second baseman Danny Murtaugh wasn't able to get out of
the way and suffered a fractured skull. Maglie
confessed that his favorite target was Dodgers'
catcher Roy Campanella because he was easily
intimidated. The Barber retired in 1958 with a
119–62 record. Most hitters were relieved.

5. EARLY WYNN

Early Wynn, winner of 300 games, once boasted that he would knock down his own grandmother if she dug in on him. During batting practice, Wynn let his fifteen-year-old son take a few swings. After the youngster hit two balls hard, dad dusted him on the third pitch. Mickey Mantle once hit a ball up the middle, narrowly missing Wynn. Early motioned his first baseman behind Mantle and repeatedly threw at Mickey's legs.

6. BURLEIGH GRIMES

Burleigh Grimes was known as "Ol' Stubblebeard" because he didn't shave on the days he pitched. It was said that Grimes's idea of an intentional walk was four pitches aimed at the batter's head. He threw at Frankie Frisch almost every time he faced him and once tried to hit Goose Goslin while he was kneeling in the on-deck circle.

7. BOB GIBSON

Cardinals' ace Bob Gibson was total business when he was on the mound. He never became friendly with opposing players because in his words, "It doesn't make sense to make friends with a guy I plan to knock down or strike out." When friend Bill White was traded to Philadelphia, Gibson dusted him. Gibson hit San Francisco third baseman Jim Ray Hart in his second major league at-bat and broke his collarbone.

8. CHICK FRASER

Chick Fraser was a pitcher with spotty control who led the league in walks in 1896, 1901, and 1905 (National League in 1896 and 1905 and American League in 1901). Fraser hit a record 217 batters, one every fifteen innings. The man with the record for hit batsmen did throw a no-hitter in 1903.

9. PINK HAWLEY

Pink Hawley set the National League record with 195 hit batsmen in only nine seasons (1892–1900). In 1895, his best season, Hawley won thirty-two games for Pittsburgh.

10. LARRY SHERRY

From 1959 to 1962, pitcher Larry Sherry and catcher Norm Sherry formed a brother battery in Los Angeles. When Larry dusted his brother during an intersquad game, Norm yelled, "I'm going to tell mom."

Beaned in Boston

Players are hit by pitches for many reasons. Some hitters crowd the plate. Others are victims of pitchers' wildness. Often the player has hit one too many home runs off the pitcher. If a pitcher wants to hit a batter bad enough, there's little the hitter can do, although Browns' outfielder Willard Brown once dragged a mattress to the plate for protection. Take aim at some of baseball's favorite targets.

1. RON HUNT

Ron Hunt proudly proclaimed, "Some people give their bodies to science. I give mine to baseball." The second baseman set a major league record by being hit fifty times in 1971. He led the National League in that department seven times, and his career total of 243 is a league record. Hunt tied a record by getting plunked 3 times in a game.

2. DON BAYLOR

Don Baylor slugged 338 home runs in his career and paid for it by being hit a record 267 times. His 35 beanings in 1986 is an American League record.

3. MINNIE MINOSO

Minnie Minoso could do it all on the field, including getting hit by pitches. Minoso led the American League a record ten times in being hit. From 1951 to 1961, he led the league every year except 1955, when he missed some games after having his skull fractured by a Bob Grim pitch.

4. FRANK ROBINSON

Frank Robinson was the ideal candidate to be a target for pitches. He crowded the plate, and he was one of the greatest home run hitters (586, fourth all-time) in baseball history. As a result, Robinson was hit 198 times and led the league in that category seven times. The only thing that kept him from further punishment was that he seemed to hit better after he was knocked down.

5. FRANKIE CROSETTI

Frankie Crosetti was the Yankees' shortstop for seventeen seasons before the arrival of Phil Rizzuto. Crosetti led the American League in being hit by pitches eight times.

6. FRANK CHANCE

The Chicago first baseman had the dubious distinction of being hit a record five times in a double header on May 30, 1904. Chance once developed a blood clot on the brain and another time was beaned so severely that he lost his hearing.

7. DON ZIMMER

Don Zimmer suffered two of the most severe beanings in baseball history. A promising minor leaguer who was leading the American Association in homers, Zimmer was playing for St. Paul when he was beaned by pitcher Jim Kirk on July 7, 1953. He was unconscious for three weeks and couldn't speak for six. Four screws were inserted into his skull to help it mend. In July 1956, Zimmer was playing Brooklyn when he was hit in the head by Cincinnati pitcher Hal Jeffcoat and suffered a fractured cheekbone and was nearly blinded. Because Zimmer froze when a pitch sailed toward him, even Sal Maglie was afraid to throw at him.

8. STEVE EVANS

St. Louis outfielder Steve Evans set the major league mark for left-handed batters when he was hit thirty-one times during the 1910 season.

9. JOE ADCOCK

Milwaukee Braves' first baseman hit 336 home runs during his career. Adcock was the first player to hit a home run into the distant centerfield bleachers at the Polo Grounds, a blast of nearly 500 feet. On July 31, 1954, Adcock set a record with eighteen total bases (four homers and a double) in a game against Brooklyn. The next day Dodgers' pitcher Clem Labine beaned Adcock. A month later, Brooklyn pitcher Don Newcombe broke Adcock's hand with a fastball, ending his season. The next year Giants' pitcher Jim Hearn broke Adcock's arm. On July 17, 1956, Adcock was brushed back by Giants' hurler Ruben Gomez. When he charged the mound, Gomez threw the ball at his legs and ran for his life. The lumbering first baseman chased Gomez all over the field until the pitcher disappeared into the clubhouse where he huddled with a bat and an ice pick in case Adcock discovered where he was hiding.

10. WILLARD SCHMIDT

Cincinnati pitcher Willard Schmidt is the only player to ever be hit by a pitch twice in the same inning. It happened in a game played against Milwaukee on April 26, 1959. To make matters worse, Schmidt had to leave the game after being hit with a drive off the bat of shortstop Johnny Logan.

Error of Their Ways

A rt Irwin is credited with being the first player to wear a glove. Considering his .856 fielding percentage, he was not the first to learn how to use one. Cincinnati second baseman Charles Smith made eighty-eight errors in only eighty games in 1880. Hall of Fame pitcher Tim Keefe made sixty-three errors in a season. Alexander Gardner once allowed twelve passed balls in a game. Dandelion Pfeffer made 828 errors in his career. When these players took the field, the defense rested.

1. ANDY LEONARD

On June 14, 1876, Boston second baseman Andy Leonard made nine errors in a 20–5 loss to Philadelphia. Leonard wisely moved to the out-field for most of the rest of his career.

2. HERMAN LONG

It was written that Herman Long played shortstop like "a man on a flying trapeze." Apparently he fell sometimes. Long made 1,037 errors, the most in major league history. In 1889 alone he made 117 miscues.

3. BILL SHINDLE

Bill Shindle, shortstop for the 1890 Philadelphia Quakers of the Players' League, set a single season record for futility when he made 122 errors.

4. MIKE GRADY

Incredibly, in 1899, third baseman Mike Grady of the New York Giants made four errors in one play. He began his comedy of errors by booting an easy grounder. Grady compounded his error by throwing wildly to first base. The runner rounded second and headed for third knowing Grady was there. Grady dropped the throw for error number three. The runner scored when Grady threw the ball into the grandstand for error number four.

5. PIANO LEGS HICKMAN

Charles "Piano Legs" Hickman of the New York Giants set a record for errors at third base with ninety-one in 1900. His fielding percentage was a dismal .842.

6. JOHN GOCHNAUR

Shortstop John Gochnaur was the original double threat man. His .185 batting average for both 1902 and 1903 were the two lowest for any player with over 400 at-bats. In 1903, his final season in the majors, he made ninety-eight errors, the twentieth-century single season record.

7. RABBIT GLAVIANO

On May 18, 1950, St. Louis Cardinals' third baseman Tommy "Rabbit" Glaviano made three consecutive errors in the ninth inning of a game against Brooklyn. His miscues, two wild throws and a boot, allowed the winning run to score in a 9–8 loss.

8. SHORTY FULLER

Washington shortstop Shorty Fuller made four errors in an inning in a game against Indianapolis on August 17, 1888. His errors allowed six runs to score, and he was removed from the game. His replacement, George Shoch, made two more errors that permitted the winning runs to score in a 11–7 loss.

9. **DICK STUART**

Dick Stuart was probably the worst fielding first baseman in baseball history. He led the league in errors at that position seven straight years from 1958 to 1964. As a rookie he made the most errors even though he played only sixty-four games. His ineptitude earned him the nickname "Dr. Strangeglove." When he was traded to Boston in 1963, Stuart belted forty-two home runs but also made twenty-nine errors. The fans in Boston once cheered when he picked up a piece of paper blowing across the field. Demoted to the minors in 1969, Stuart showed he hadn't lost his touch by leading the Pacific Coast League with 22 errors in less than half a season.

10. **"BANANA NOSE" ZEKE BONURA**

Perhaps the only man who could rival Dick Stuart as the worst defensive first baseman of all time was "Banana Nose" Zeke Bonura. Like Stuart, Banana Nose could hit the ball a mile and kick it even farther. Humorist Jean Shepherd recalled that Bonura had a range of "about six inches." Routine grounders would roll by as Bonura gave his "Mussolini Salute" with his glove. His specialty was calling the pitcher off a play and losing the race to the bag with the runner.

Mismanagement

It has often been said that managers are only as good as the players they have to work with. It can also be said that teams are only as good as their managers. On anyone's scorecard these managers must rank among the least successful in baseball history.

1. GUY HECKER

Guy Hecker was a spectacular player. In 1884 he won fifty-two games while pitching for Louisville of the American Association. Two years later Hecker batted .342 to become the only pitcher in baseball history to win a batting title. On August 15, 1886, he scored a record seven runs, hit three home runs, had six hits, and pitched a four-hitter. Hecker's gifts did not extend to managing. In 1890, he managed Pittsburgh to a 23–113 record.

2. JOE QUINN

A mortician in the off-season, Australian-born Joe Quinn usually had whatever team he managed buried in the cellar. He had a brief trial at the helm in St. Louis in 1895, winning thirteen and losing twenty-seven. Four years later, he managed the talent-depleted Cleveland Spiders to a 20–134 record, the worst in baseball history. Under Quinn's inspired guidance, the Spiders lost forty of their last forty-one games.

3. CHARLIE GOULD

In the National League's first season, 1876, Charlie Gould managed Cincinnati to a 9–56 record. Gould was fired as manager, although he did continue to play first base for Cincinnati for another season.

4. DOC PROTHRO

For sheer consistency, Doc Prothro deserves recognition in any discussion of bad managers. Doc piloted the Phillies to three consecutive last place finishes from 1939 to 1941. Never winning more than fifty games, his overall record was 138–320. When he wasn't losing games as a manager, Doc practiced dentistry in the off-season.

5. **JACK AND DAVE ROWE**

It's hard to decide which of the Rowe brothers, Jack or Dave, was the least successful manager. Jack Rowe managed Buffalo of the Players League to a 36–96 record in 1890. Brother Dave, who once gave up thirty-five runs in a game as a pitcher, had a career 44–126 record in two stints as manager of Kansas City in 1886 and 1888.

6. **CHICKEN WOLF**

The 1889 Louisville team was one of the worst of all time. Four managers guided the team to a 27–111 record, including twenty-six consecutive losses. During his stint, Chicken Wolf managed the team to a 15–51 mark. En route to Philadelphia, the team arrived in Johnstown, Pennsylvania, just in time for the legendary Johnstown Flood, which claimed 2,200 lives. It was thought that the team had perished, but fortunately for the rest of the league, they had found high ground and were unharmed.

7. **HORACE FOGEL**

Horace Fogel was a sportswriter who managed Indianapolis in 1887 to a 20–49 record. Fifteen years later, he managed the New York Giants for forty-one games before being replaced by Heinie Smith. While with the Giants, Fogel came up with the brilliant suggestion that pitcher Christy Mathewson be converted to a first baseman. His successor, Heinie Smith, lost twenty-seven of thirty-two games before being fired. Smith had the brainstorm to make Mathewson a shortstop. His replacement, John McGraw, put Matty on the mound, where he won 372 games in a Giants' uniform. McGraw, one of the greatest managers in major league history, guided the Giants to ten pennants.

8. JIMMY DYKES

Jimmy Dykes managed six different teams between 1934 and 1961. His twenty-one years of managing without winning a pennant or division title is a record. Dykes's teams never finished higher than third place.

9. ROGERS HORNSBY

A lifetime .358 hitter, Rogers Hornsby was arguably the greatest second baseman of all time. In 1926, his St. Louis Cardinals won the world championship while he served as a player-manager. However, nine of the thirteen years he managed, his teams finished in the second division. Hornsby had a less than ideal rapport with his players. Once, while managing in the minors, Hornsby went into the shower and urinated on a pitcher who had been knocked out of the box.

10. **PONGO CANILLON**

Joe "Pongo" Canillon managed Washington from 1907 to 1909. In two of the three seasons, his team finished in the cellar, and Pongo was fired after his team finished 42–110 in 1909. His career record as manager was 158 wins and 297 losses.

Travelin' Men

Some players just seem to be always passing through. Harry Simpson, an outfielder who played in the 1950s, was given the nickname "Suitcase" because he was traded so often. Pitcher Mike Ryba played in seventeen different minor leagues before he reached the majors in 1935.

1. BOBO NEWSOM

Between 1929 and 1953, Bobo Newsom changed uniforms seventeen different times. Three times Newsom was a twenty-game winner and three times he led the league in losses. He never played more than two full seasons with the same club. Newsom had five different stints with Washington because it was rumored that owner Clark Griffith enjoyed playing pinochle with him.

2. CHARLES "POP" SMITH

Infielder Charles "Pop" Smith played for eleven different teams in two leagues during his career, which lasted from 1880 to 1891. He saw action for Cincinnati, Cleveland, Worcester, Buffalo, and Boston of the National League, and Philadelphia, Baltimore, Louisville, Columbus, Pittsburgh, and Washington of the American Association.

3. TOMMY DAVIS

Tommy Davis won batting titles while playing for the Los Angeles Dodgers in 1962 and 1963. After spending his first eight seasons in Los Angeles, Davis played for the Mets, Astros, Cubs, White Sox, Pilots, A's, Orioles, Angels, and Royals.

4. DICK LITTLEFIELD

Pitcher Dick Littlefield was known as the "Marco Polo of Baseball." During his nine years in the majors (1950–58), Littlefield played for nine different clubs in ten different cities. In 1956, he was traded to the Dodgers for Jackie Robinson, but the trade was voided when Robinson retired. It's hard to understand why he was so much in demand, considering his 33–54 lifetime record.

5. MIKE MORGAN

At last count, pitcher Mike Morgan had played for eleven different major league clubs and a total of

Tommy Davis
Despite winning batting titles in 1962 and 1963, Tommy Davis played for ten different teams in the major leagues.

twenty professional teams. Morgan has made stops in Oakland, New York (Yankees), Toronto, Seattle, Baltimore, Los Angeles, Chicago (Cubs), St. Louis, Cincinnati, Minnesota, and Texas.

6. BOB MILLER

Pitcher Bob Miller played for ten different teams during his career, which lasted from 1957 to 1974. During a four-year period (1970–73), he played for seven different teams.

7. DIRTY JACK DOYLE

During his seventeen-year career (1889–1905), Dirty Jack Doyle played every position except pitcher. It seemed as though he played for almost every team. Doyle appeared in the uniforms of ten different teams.

8. KEN BRETT

Ken Brett, brother of superstar third baseman George Brett, pitched for ten different teams between 1971 and 1980. Brett was the youngest pitcher (age nineteen) to appear in a World Series and set another record for a pitcher by hitting home runs in four consecutive games.

9. GEORGE BRUNET

Lefty George Brunet played for nine different teams in his fifteen years (1956–71) in the majors. He led the American League in losses in 1967 and 1968 but was not traded either of those years.

10. TED GRAY

Pitcher Ted Gray would have qualified for frequent flier miles if they had existed in 1955. Despite only appearing in fourteen games that season, Gray played for four different teams: White Sox, Indians, Yankees, and Orioles.

Baseball's Worst Trades

A trade that is terrible for one team is great for another. The following transactions are the biggest steals in baseball history.

Milt Pappas
The Cincinnati Reds made one of the worst deals in baseball history in 1965 when they traded slugger Frank Robinson to Baltimore for pitcher Milt Pappas.

1. **BABE RUTH**

Babe Ruth was playing for Baltimore of the International League in 1914 when club owner Jack Dunn attempted to sell him to a major league team. Dunn offered Ruth, pitcher Ernie Shore (who later pitched a perfect game), and catcher Ben Egan to Connie Mack for $10,000. The financially strapped owner of the Philadelphia Athletics reluctantly declined. Cincinnati had an option to acquire two players from the Orioles. The Reds sent an inexperienced scout named Harry Stevens who passed over Ruth and Shore for outfielder George Twombly and shortstop Claude Derrick. Neither Twombly nor Derrick ever hit a home run for Cincinnati, while Ruth, of course, hit 714 in his illustrious career.

2. **CHRISTY MATHEWSON FOR AMOS RUSIE**

Amos Rusie was the hardest throwing pitcher of the nineteenth century. Five times the "Hoosier Thunderbolt" led the National League in strike-outs. Although the eight-time twenty-game winner had not pitched in two years, Cincinnati was glad to acquire him in exchange for an untested pitcher named Christy Mathewson. Washed up, Rusie only pitched three games for Cincinnati, giving up forty-four hits in twenty-three innings. Mathewson became the best pitcher in the

National League and won 372 games for the Giants.

3. FRANK ROBINSON FOR MILT PAPPAS

Cincinnati fans were devastated in 1965 when Reds owner Bill DeWitt traded slugger Frank Robinson to Baltimore for pitchers Milt Pappas and Jack Baldschun and outfielder Dick Simpson. DeWitt justified the trade by calling Robinson an "old thirty." In 1966, Robinson won the Triple Crown, and Baltimore won the world championship. Pappas won thirty games in Cincinnati in three seasons before being dealt to Atlanta.

4. NOLAN RYAN FOR JIM FREGOSI

In December 1971, the New York Mets acquired infielder Jim Fregosi from the California Angels. They sent the Angels four players: Don Rose, Leroy Stanton, Francisco Estrada, and Nolan Ryan. Fregosi played a little over a year in New York before being sent to Texas. Nolan Ryan won 324 games, pitched seven no-hitters and became baseball's all-time strikeout leader with 5,714.

5. JOE DIMAGGIO

Joe DiMaggio could have been the Cub Clipper. Chicago had the opportunity to purchase the talented outfielder but declined because they were wary of a knee injury that DiMaggio had suffered getting out of a car in 1934. DiMaggio joined the New York Yankees in 1936 and became an instant star.

6. LOU BROCK FOR ERNIE BROGLIO

In June 1964, the St. Louis Cardinals traded former twenty-game winners Ernie Broglio and Bobby Shantz along with Doug Clemens for Jack Spring, Paul Toth, and a young outfielder named Lou Brock. Shantz never won a game in Chicago, and Broglio had a miserable 14–31 record with the Cubs. Brock led the Cardinals to world championships in 1964 and 1967 and finished his Hall of Fame career with more than 3,000 base hits.

7. STEVE CARLTON FOR RICK WISE

The Cardinals were on the short end of the stick in 1972 when they traded lefthanded pitcher Steve Carlton to Philadelphia for righthander Rick Wise. Wise won thirty-two games over two years in St. Louis before being shipped to Boston. Carlton won four Cy Young Awards in Philadelphia and became the second winningest lefthander in baseball history with 329.

8. ROCKY COLAVITO FOR HARVEY KUENN

Cleveland fans were horrified in April 1960 when fan favorite Rocky Colavito was traded to Detroit for Harvey Kuenn. Colavito, who led the American League in home runs in 1959, smashed 139 home runs in four seasons in Detroit. Kuenn, the 1959 American League batting champion, played only one season in Cleveland. Many Tribe fans believe that the trade brought a curse on the team, which did not win another pennant for thirty-four years.

9. FERGUSON JENKINS FOR LARRY JACKSON

The Phillies thought they had acquired pitching help in 1966 when they received veteran right-handers Larry Jackson and Bob Buhl from the Cubs for rookie pitcher Ferguson Jenkins and

Larry Jackson
Larry Jackson had a losing season after being traded to the Philadelphia Phillies for pitcher Ferguson Jenkins who went on to have six 20-win seasons for the Chicago Cubs.

outfielders Adolfo Phillips and John Herrnstein.
Jackson, who led the National League with twenty-
four wins in 1964, had a losing record in Philadelphia. Buhl was 6–8 in 1966, then retired. Ferguson
Jenkins won twenty games six seasons in a row
for the Cubs.

10. RYNE SANDBERG FOR IVAN DE JESUS

The Cubs made another steal in 1982 when they
traded shortstop Ivan De Jesus to Philadelphia for
veteran shortstop Larry Bowa and rookie infielder
Ryne Sandberg. Both De Jesus and Bowa played
three full seasons for their respective teams, but
Sandberg became a perennial All-Star second
baseman.

Baseball's Weirdest Trades

Everybody hears about the blockbuster trades teams make, but for every big deal there are many lesser ones. You'll agree that these are some of the strangest trades ever made.

1. LINDY CHAPPOTEN

Minor league pitcher Lindy Chappoten was once traded in exchange for twenty uniforms. It proved to be a bargain as he went on to win twenty games.

2. TIM FORTUGNO

Tim Fortugno struck out twenty-four batters in a minor league game for El Paso. In 1989, the Reno Red Sox sold Fortugno to the Milwaukee Brewers for cash and twelve dozen baseballs. Fortugno never pitched a game in Milwaukee.

3. ERNIE HARWELL

In 1948, Brooklyn Dodgers' Branch Rickey wanted to secure the services of a minor league announcer named Ernie Harwell. He sent minor league catcher Cliff Dapper to the Atlanta Crackers in exchange for Harwell. The venerable Harwell became a fixture in the broadcasting booth, most notably spending over three decades announcing games in Detroit. Dapper is also an interesting story. Despite hitting .471 during a brief trial in Brooklyn in 1942, he was never given another chance to catch in the major leagues.

4. LOU BOUDREAU FOR CHARLIE GRIMM

On May 4, 1960, the Chicago Cubs traded manager Charlie Grimm for one of their announcers, Lou Boudreau, who had led the Cleveland Indians to the world championship in 1948 as a player-manager. After managing the Cubs to a 54–83 mark, Boudreau returned to broadcasting. Cubs owner Phil Wrigley replaced him with a college of coaches in which several coaches shared the responsibilities of managing.

5. CLIFF HEATHCOTE FOR MAX FLACK

The Chicago Cubs played a doubleheader against the St. Louis Cardinals on May 30, 1922. Between games, the Cardinals traded outfielder Cliff Heathcote to the Cubs for outfielder Max Flack. Both players were hitless in the first game, but each had hits in the nightcap for their new teams.

6. HARRY CHITI

On April 26, 1962, the Cleveland Indians traded catcher Harry Chiti to the New York Mets for a player to be named later. A few weeks later the Mets sent Chiti back to Cleveland as the player to be named later. In essence Harry Chiti was traded for himself.

7. DICK COFFMAN FOR CARL FISCHER

The St. Louis Browns traded pitcher Dick Coffman to the Washington Senators for pitcher Carl Fischer on June 9, 1932. Six months later, the Senators traded Coffman back to the Browns for Fischer. Coffman was 1–6 during his brief stay in Washington, and Fischer was 3–7 while playing for St. Louis.

8. JOEL YOUNGBLOOD

Joel Youngblood became the only major leaguer to get a base hit for two different teams in the same day. On August 4, 1982, Youngblood, play-ing for the New York Mets, singled off Chicago Cubs' pitcher Ferguson Jenkins. That afternoon he was traded to Montreal. He arrived in

Philadelphia in time to play an evening game against the Phillies and hit a pinch single off Steve Carlton. Youngblood had gotten base hits off two future Hall of Fame pitchers in the same day in different uniforms.

9. MURRAY WALL FOR DICK HYDE

In 1959, Boston pitcher Murray Wall was traded to Washington for reliever Dick Hyde. Wall appeared in a game for Washington before learning that the trade had been canceled because Hyde had a sore arm.

10. "THREE FINGER" BROWN

For two seasons the Federal League competed against the established National and American Leagues. The Federal League folded in 1916. In February of that year, the Chicago franchise of the Federal League traded Mordecai "Three Finger" Brown, Joe Tinker, Clem Clemens, Mickey Doolan, Bill Fischer, Max Flack, Claude Hendrix, Les Mann, Dykes Potter, Rollie Zeider, and George McConnell to the Chicago Cubs for cash.

Outrageous Owners

Until the era of free agency, the owners had the upper hand in dealings with players. Pittsburgh owner Barney Dreyfuss argued with Dick Bartell over the cost of a lobster dinner, eventually deducting $2.40 from the shortstop's paycheck. When a fan made off with rookie shortstop Phil Rizzuto's cap, the Yankees made him pay for it. Detroit owner Frank Nevin froze Ty Cobb's salary at $9,000 for three years even though he was winning the batting title every season. Let me introduce you to some of baseball's most outrageous owners.

1. BILL VEECK

Baseball's most imaginative owner, Bill Veeck, will be remembered for his amazing stunts. As a minor league owner in Milwaukee, he once had a new pitcher jump out of manager Charlie Grimm's birthday cake. In 1948, his Cleveland Indians won the world championship while drawing a record 2,620,627 fans. That year fans were outraged when word leaked out that Veeck was considering trading star shortstop Lou Boudreau to St. Louis. Veeck went from bar to bar to personally apologize to the fans.

Some of his most memorable moments came as owner of the financially strapped St. Louis Browns. In 1951, he sent midget Eddie Gaedel to the plate in a game against Detroit. A few days later, he staged Grandstand Manager's Night in which a thousand fans holding YES and NO placards decided the strategy for the game. As manager Zack Taylor sat idly in a rocking chair, the fans managed the hapless Browns to a 5–3 victory. What made Veeck's stunts even more effective is that he rarely announced them ahead of time. If a fan did not attend a game, he was always in danger of missing something unusual and entertaining.

Veeck owned the White Sox twice, and each time left his unique mark. When the "Go Go Sox" (so called because of their emphasis on speed) won the American League pennant in 1959, he once again hired Eddie Gaedel, this time to dress up like a Martian and "capture" the Sox double-play combination of Nellie Fox and Luis Aparicio. While in Chicago he also introduced the exploding

scoreboard in 1960 and the infamous Disco Demolition Night in 1979, which resulted in a riot after
fans built bonfires with disco records. To Veeck's
credit, he tried to break baseball's color barrier in
1943 by buying the Philadelphia Phillies and signing the best Negro League players. When that plan
was foiled, he later signed Larry Doby, who became the first African American to play in the
American League.

2. CHARLIE O. FINLEY

Pitcher Mike Torrez called owner Charlie O. Finley
the "Wizard of Odd." Finley's tenure as owner of
the A's was always eventful. In Kansas City, he
made a jackass, which he named Charlie O. after
himself, the mascot. Fond of farmyard animals,
he forced the players to enter the stadium on a
mule team and had sheep grazing beyond the
outfield fence. A mechanical rabbit delivered the
baseballs to the umpire.

When the team moved to Oakland, Finley
offered $300 to players who would grow handle-
bar mustaches. In their Kelly green and gold uniforms and white shoes, the "Swingin' A's" were
instantly recognizable. Finley went too far when
he asked pitcher Vida Blue to change his name to
True Blue. Vida, whose name means life, was
named after his father. Blue suggested, "Why
doesn't he change his name to True Finley?"

A hatred of Finley was the uniting force for the players. During the 1973 World Series, Finley tried to put Mike Andrews on the disabled list after he made two costly errors. Despite the turmoil, the Oakland A's won three consecutive championships from 1972 to 1974.

3. **MARGE SCHOTT**

The controversial owner of the Cincinnati Reds has endured two suspensions for insensitive remarks concerning blacks, Jews, gays, and other minorities. She reportedly referred to outfielder Eric Davis as her "million dollar nigger." Marge warned her players not to accessorize because, in her words, "only fruits wear earrings." Her cost-cutting measures included selling the general manager's seat at Cinergy Field and briefly refusing to show scores from other games because it cost $200 a month. Classic Marge moments include giving year-old candy to employees at Christmas and presenting umpires with recycled flowers after the death of umpire John McSherry on Opening Day. Schott's pride and joy was her beloved St. Bernard Schottzie. She rubbed Schottzie hair on her players for good luck and printed a ticket calendar that featured twelve photos of the dog in various poses, such as Santa and Miss Liberty.

4. GEORGE STEINBRENNER

Johnny Carson joked, "There are close to eleven million unemployed, and half of them are Yankee managers." For the past quarter-century Stein-brenner has been in charge of the "Bronx Zoo." Over an eleven-year period, there were fourteen managerial changes. Billy Martin had five separate stints at the Yankee helm. Dick Howser was fired after winning 103 games in 1980. In 1982 alone the Yankees had five pitching coaches and three batting instructors.

Steinbrenner was suspended in 1974 after being convicted of making an illegal $100,000 contribution to the reelection committee for President Richard Nixon. The "Boss" was suspended indefinitely after it became known that he had paid gambler Howard Spira $40,000 to try to dig up dirt on outfielder Dave Winfield. For all his faults, Steinbrenner has presided over four world champion teams (1977, 1978, 1996, and 1998).

5. CHRIS VON DER AHE

Chris Von der Ahe was the nineteenth-century version of George Steinbrenner. "Der Boss," as the German-born owner of the St. Louis Browns was known, ordered thirty-two managerial changes in only seventeen years. Between 1895 and 1897, he changed managers twelve times. Like Marge Schott, he brought his dogs (greyhounds named Schnauzer and Snoozer) to the ballpark. Like Charlie Finley, his team wore multicolored silk uniforms. Baseball's first showman, he staged horse races and Wild West shows in the outfield.

Von der Ahe could attract a crowd on his own. He was a potbellied man with a nose that was described as looking like a "bunch of strawberries." He wore loud checkered suits, spats, and diamond stickpins. "Der Boss" owned a saloon near the ballpark and bought the team mainly to increase his bar profits. Von der Ahe sat in the dugout, viewing the game through a telescope. He encouraged players to get into fights and stomped on an umpire's feet until they were bloody. When it became too dark to play, Von der Ahe once placed candles in front of the dugout, starting a fire.

In 1898, Von der Ahe was ruined when the ballpark did burn down, and he went through a costly divorce. To make matters worse, Pittsburgh owner William Nimick had Von der Ahe kidnapped by private detectives and jailed because of an old debt. He died destitute, and former manager Charles Comiskey paid for his funeral. Despite the buffoonery, Von der Ahe's Browns won four consecutive American Association pennants between 1885 and 1888.

6. ANDREW FREEDMAN

Probably the most hated owner in baseball history, Andrew Freedman nearly destroyed the New York Giants' franchise during his reign of terror from 1895 to 1902. He took over a team that had finished forty-four games over .500 in 1894, and in one year the team sank from second to ninth place. Only once did his team finish above seventh place. The Giants had thirteen managers in seven years.

A politician in the infamous Tammany Hall, Freedman carried on feuds with everyone from sportswriters to owners. Backed by his own storm troopers, he beat up players, umpires, fans, and even owners. If umpires made calls that displeased him, he would not allow them into the Polo Grounds. He got involved in a bitter dispute with Amos Rusie that caused the star pitcher to sit out a season. The Giants finished last in 1902, Freedman's last as owner. The next season they finished second, and a year later they won the pennant.

7. JOHN TAYLOR

After inheriting the Boston Red Sox in 1904, John Taylor began dismantling the championship team. He traded batting champion George Stone to St. Louis and future home run king Gavvy

Cravath to Chicago. He dealt baseball's winningest pitcher Cy Young to Cleveland after Taylor had an all-night drinking session with owner Charles Somers. Although he knew almost nothing about baseball, he insisted on lecturing his players. Two years after winning the 1904 pennant, Boston lost 105 games and sank to last place.

8. CHARLES COMISKEY

If Chicago White Sox owner Charles Comiskey had not been such a tightwad, the Black Sox Scandal might never had occurred. In 1908, star pitcher Ed Walsh was paid $3,500 and became the last pitcher to win forty games in a season. Expecting a large raise, Walsh was pleased Comiskey handed him a check for $3,500 in appreciation of his brilliant season. Walsh assumed it was a bonus. He was stunned to receive a contract for the 1909 season for the same salary as the previous year. Only after he threatened to hold out, was he able to get a $1,500 bonus.

The 1919 White Sox were grossly underpaid. The Sox had won the 1917 World Series, but only second baseman Eddie Collins was fairly compensated. Pitcher Eddie Cicotte had led the American League in wins (28) and earned run average (1.53) in 1917, yet his salary for 1919 was only $3,500.

He had an incentive clause that would pay him $5,000 if he won thirty. Cicotte had twenty-nine wins with three weeks to go in the season when Comiskey ordered him not to pitch anymore. Comiskey said that he wanted Cicotte rested for the World Series, but Cicotte knew he was just trying to get out of paying the $1,500 bonus. So when gamblers offered Cicotte and the others $10,000 to throw the series, it's understandable why they accepted. Comiskey was so cheap that he let the team play in dirty uniforms until the players paid for the cleaning.

Perhaps Comiskey's most unforgivable act concerned pitcher Dickie Kerr. He had been one of the honest White Sox and won two games in the series. Kerr won twenty-one games in 1920 and nineteen games the next year. The miserly Comiskey offered Kerr $3,500. Kerr decided to accept an offer of $5,000 from a semipro team and was suspended from baseball. He met the same fate as his crooked teammates.

9. RAY KROC

Ray Kroc made his fortune creating the McDonald's hamburger chain. He bought the San Diego Padres in 1974. At their first home game on April 19, 1974, the Padres were being clobbered by Houston 9–2 in the eighth inning when Kroc grabbed the microphone and said, "I've never seen such stupid baseball playing in my life." Encouraged by his constructive criticism, the Padres lost 102 games that year. Kroc later admitted, "Baseball has brought me nothing but aggravation—it can go to hell." When asked about the future of the national pastime, Kroc said, "There's a lot more future in hamburgers than in baseball." Kroc died in January 1984. The Padres, free of Kroc's obtrusive ownership, went on to win their first pennant in 1984.

10. CALVIN GRIFFITH

Calvin Griffith made some comments that would even make Marge Schott blush. Griffith owned the Washington Senators and moved the franchise to Minnesota in 1964. Griffith explained that one of the reasons he made the move was that Washington, D. C. had too many African Americans and that they rarely attended games. He told the fans in Minnesota, "We came here because you've got good hard-working white people here." Griffith attributed a slump of catcher Butch Wynegar to his recent marriage. He suggested that one-night stands would have given him more time to concentrate on baseball. Pitcher Jim Kaat remarked that Griffith was so cheap that he "threw quarters around like manhole covers." Griffith may have best summed up his philosophy when he said, "I can't tell you what I intend to do. But I can tell you one thing: it won't be anything rational."

Worst Promotions

Since the days of Chris Von der Ahe, promotional gimmicks have been used by baseball to entice fans to the ballpark. Although many promotions have been successful, a few can only be described as disastrous.

1. TEN-CENT BEER NIGHT

On June 4, 1974, the Cleveland Indians staged a ten-cent beer night. After all, beer and baseball had been synonymous for a century. The lure of cheap beer brought a crowd of 25,134 thirsty fans to the game against the Texas Rangers. Over 65,000 glasses of dime beer were sold. As the evening progressed, the fans, saturated with beer, became rowdier. Drunken fans were pelting the bull pen with beer, firecrackers, and smoke bombs. The game was tied 5–5 in the ninth inning when a fan jumped out of the stands and tried to grab

Texas outfielder Jeff Burroughs's cap. Fans began pouring out into the field, attacking players and umpires. Pitcher Tom Hilgendorf and umpire Nestor Chylak were hit over the head with folding chairs, and several other players were injured. The game was forfeited to Texas.

2. DISCO DEMOLITION NIGHT

Chicago White Sox owner Bill Veeck decided to mark the end of the disco craze with Disco Demolition Night on July 12, 1979. While his intentions may have been noble, the result was nearly catastrophic. More than 50,000 fans paid the 98 cent admission for the opportunity to destroy the despised disco records. Overenthusiastic fans began tossing the discs onto the field like Frisbees. As a bonfire fueled by disco records commenced, over 5,000 fans ran onto the field. When they wouldn't return to their seats, the game was forfeited to Detroit.

3. ARMY DAY

On June 10, 1975, the Yankees (who were playing in Shea Stadium while Yankee Stadium was being renovated) held Army Day in honor of the armed services' two hundredth birthday. The highlight of the ceremony was an ear-splitting cannon barrage. When the smoke cleared, fans were stunned to see that the blast had shattered windows and blown away a section of the center-field fence.

4. SCRAP IRON DAY

During World War II, salvage drives at the ballpark were a common occurrence. On September 26, 1942, 11,000 youngsters were admitted free to the Polo Grounds for a game between the Giants and the Braves because they brought some metal for the war effort. With the Giants leading 5–2 in the eighth inning, the children began invading the field. Umpire Ziggy Sears, unable to restore order, forfeited the game to Boston.

5. GOOD OLD JOE EARLY NIGHT

Joe Early, a night watchman in Cleveland, wrote owner Bill Veeck in 1948 complaining that there were no nights to honor fans. Veeck responded by announcing a night in honor of Joe Early. At Good Old Joe Early night, the fan was presented with an outhouse, a backfiring model T, and some livestock. Besides the gag gifts, Early received a Ford convertible, appliances, and a watch.

6. THE SAN FRANCISCO CRAB

With the success of the San Diego Chicken, other teams attempted to develop their own mascots.

The San Francisco Giants conducted a poll to see what kind of mascot their fans preferred. Two-thirds of those who answered indicated they didn't want any at all. Undaunted, the Giants chose a crab. The mascot, introduced in 1984, looked as though it had just climbed from under a rock. It slithered across the field, threatening to give seafood a bad name. Fans responded by spitting on the monstrosity and pouring beer on it.

7. **MR. RED**

Cincinnati's answer to the San Francisco Crab was a mascot known as Mr. Red. Dressed in a Reds uniform, Mr. Red's head was a huge baseball. During a rally, he would stand atop the dugout attempting to whip the fans into a frenzy. Unfortunately, few of the fans could see what was happening because they were blocked by Mr. Red's enormous head. Eventually Mr. Red was retired, to the relief of box seat holders.

8. **RANDY MYERS POSTER DAY**

During the early 1990s, the Chicago Cubs had poster giveaway days honoring their best players. On Randy Myers Day, fans were given posters of the lefthanded reliever. Myers was not having his best day, and when he blew the lead, irate Cubs fans threw hundreds of Myers's posters onto the field.

9. HARMON KILLEBREW NIGHT

Harmon Killebrew belted 573 home runs, the most ever by a righthanded batter in the American League. After spending twenty-one years with the Washington Senators and Minnesota Twins, Killebrew was traded to Kansas City. When Kansas City visited Minnesota, Twins' owner Calvin Griffith decided to have Harmon Killebrew Night to honor the slugger. In a shameful display of indifference, fewer than 3,000 fans showed up to honor the team's greatest player.

10. BURYING THE PENNANT

In one of Bill Veeck's most bizarre promotions, the Cleveland Indians buried the 1948 pennant. During a pregame ceremony on September 23, 1949, the Indians, out of contention, formed a funeral procession. Veeck led the mourners, and manager Lou Boudreau served as a pallbearer. A cardboard tombstone marked the grave of the 1948 champs. Appropriately, the Indians were buried by the Tigers 5–0.

It's All in the Game

Anything can happen at a baseball game. Games have been called because of fog, hurricanes, and even a grasshopper invasion. In 1913, a St. Louis outfielder took a parasol onto the field after losing two fly balls in the sun. Pitcher John Clarkson once threw a lemon to demonstrate that it was too dark to continue play.

1. GROVER LAND

Keeping your eye on the ball was harder than usual at a 1915 Federal League game between the Brooklyn Tip Tops and the Baltimore Terrapins. Umpire Bill Brennan stacked the game balls in a pile behind the pitcher's mound. Brooklyn catcher Grover Land hit a ball up the middle that hit the pile of balls. They scattered all over the field like a rack of pool balls being broken. The infielders each picked up a ball and tagged the runner. Brennan, unable to determine which was the game ball, declared that Land was entitled to a home run.

2. **ABNER POWELL**

On August 22, 1886, the term "dogging it" took on a new meaning. Louisville and Cincinnati were tied 3–3 in the eleventh inning when the Colonels' Chicken Wolf hit a ball into the gap. As Cincinnati outfielder Abner Powell chased the ball, he awakened a dog that had been sleeping near the fence. The mutt grabbed Powell's trousers, and while he struggled to break free, Wolf circled the bases with the winning run.

3. **CAL MCVEY**

The Cincinnati Red Stockings, baseball's first all-professional team, brought a 130-game undefeated streak into a game against the Brooklyn Atlantics on June 14, 1870. The Red Stockings appeared to be on their way to another victory when they took a 7–5 lead in the eleventh inning. The Atlantics rallied for three runs in the bottom of the inning, thanks to an overzealous fan who jumped on the back of Cincinnati outfielder Cal McVey as he chased a fly ball.

4. CLARK GRIFFITH AND CONNIE MACK

On April 14, 1948, Clark Griffith, the seventy-eight-year-old owner of the Washington Senators, challenged Connie Mack, eighty-four-year-old owner of the Philadelphia A's, to a ninety-foot match race. The race ended in a flatfooted tie.

5. ICEBOX CHAMBERLAIN AND JOHN CLARKSON

Boston's John Clarkson and Cincinnati's Icebox Chamberlain were locked in a brilliant pitchers' duel on May 6, 1892. The game was scoreless in the fourteenth inning when play was halted by umpire Jack Sheridan because the setting sun was blinding the batters. When conditions didn't improve, Sheridan was forced to call the game on account of the sun.

6. RAINOUT AT THE ASTRODOME

Without even springing a leak, the Houston Astrodome was the site of a rainout on June 15, 1976. Seven inches of rain had flooded the streets, making it almost impossible to reach the ballpark. About twenty brave souls made it to the Astrodome. The game was canceled, and the intrepid fans were treated to a meal and given rain checks.

7. FRANK CORRIDON

New York Giants' pitcher Frank Corridon was the victim of his own fans on April 11, 1907. A freak snowstorm had hit the New York area. Corridon was pitching a shutout against Philadelphia in the eighth inning when fans began pelting the players with snowballs. The crowd was so uncontrollable that umpire Bill Klem forfeited the game to Philadelphia.

8. EDD ROUSH

Edd Roush once got ejected from a game without saying a word. On June 8, 1920, Roush was playing centerfield for Cincinnati in a game against the New York Giants at the Polo Grounds. Reds' skipper Pat Moran got into a heated argument with the umpires. As the debate raged, Roush laid down in the outfield and took a nap. Roush was so difficult to wake up that he was ejected for delaying the game.

9. FRANK PETERS

Portland manager Frank Peters took a lesson from volleyball in a Northwest League game against Tri-Cities on August 31, 1974. Peters rotated his players so that each one played a different position for an inning. The strategy worked—Portland won the game 8–7.

10. CHARLES CLANCY AND JACK CORBETT

Baseball is often criticized for the length of its games. However, Winston-Salem and Asheville once completed a North Carolina League game in thirty-one minutes. Managers Charles Clancy (Winston-Salem) and Jack Corbett (Asheville) agreed to play the August 30, 1916 game as quickly as possible so the teams could catch a train leaving at 3:00. At their managers' insistence, everyone swung at the first pitch. Once the Asheville pitcher made a pitch before his teammates had time to take the field. The transition was so confusing that the Winston-Salem centerfielder actually threw out his own teammate at second base. Winston-Salem won the game by the score of 2–1.

Baseball's Most Embarrassing Moments

Baseball can be an embarrassing game. Minor leaguer Ed Stewart once swung so hard that he knocked himself out. A hungover Pete Browning fell asleep after taking a long lead off from second base and was tagged out. Facing fireballer Walter Johnson in an exhibition game, Reds' outfielder George Harper went back to the dugout after only two strikes because he knew he couldn't hit the "Big Train's" fastball.

1. JIM ST. VRAIN

Pitcher Jim St. Vrain of the Chicago Cubs made an unbelievable baserunning blunder in a game against Pittsburgh in 1902. The weak-hitting pitcher, who normally batted righthanded, decided to try batting lefthanded to change his luck. St. Vrain hit a grounder to shortstop Honus Wagner and began running hard—down the third base line.

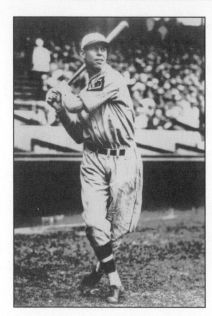

Babe Herman
Babe Herman's baserunning was so suspect that he once doubled into a double play.

2. WILBERT ROBINSON

Brooklyn manager Wilbert Robinson attempted to catch a ball dropped from an airplane. He didn't know that a grapefruit had been substituted for the baseball. When the grapefruit spattered in his glove, Robinson mistook the juice for blood. He lay on the ground moaning that he was mortally injured while the Dodgers laughed hysterically.

3. HACK WILSON

On July 4, 1934, Brooklyn manager Casey Stengel went to the mound to remove his pitcher, Boom Boom Beck, in a game at Philadelphia's Baker

Bowl. Beck, irate because he was being taken out of the game, fired the ball off the tin rightfield fence. Rightfielder Hack Wilson, who was badly hungover from a night of drinking, heard the sound of the ball hitting the wall and raced toward the fence. He retrieved the ball and made a perfect throw to second to nail the phantom runner.

4. JOSÉ CANSECO

Texas outfielder José Canseco used his head to turn a fly ball into a home run. On May 25, 1993, Canseco drifted back on a fly ball hit by Cleveland's Carlos Martinez. The ball bounced off Canseco's head and went over the fence for a home run. Four days later, Canseco tried his hand at pitching and required surgery after he blew out his right elbow.

5. LOU NOVIKOFF

Lou "the Mad Russian" Novikoff's entire career was an embarrassment. A four-time minor league batting champion, he never got the hang of major league fielding or playing the outfield in Chicago's Wrigley Field. Novikoff once stole third base with the bases loaded because, he explained, "I had such a good jump on the pitcher." His defense was even more atrocious. He claimed that he couldn't play Wrigley Field because the left field line was crooked. The Mad Russian also had a phobia about ivy and would get nowhere near the vines that covered the outfield walls at Wrigley.

6. BABE HERMAN

Babe Herman was a super hitter (.324 career batting average) who never quite got the hang of base running. His most infamous moment occurred on August 15, 1926 when Babe doubled into a double play. Herman, running with his head down, arrived at third base only to find two other Dodgers standing on the bag.

7. MARVELOUS MARV THRONEBERRY

First baseman Marv Throneberry personified the ineptitude of the original New York Mets. At manager Casey Stengel's birthday party, Throneberry asked why he wasn't given a piece of cake. Casey replied, "We'd given you a piece but we were afraid you'd drop it." Even when Marvelous Marv did something right, it turned out wrong. After hitting a triple, he was called out for missing first base. When Stengel went out to argue the call, a Mets' coach stopped him and said, "Don't bother, Casey, he missed second, too."

8. JOHNNY BENCH

During the third game of the 1972 World Series, Cincinnati catcher Johnny Bench came to bat against Oakland reliever Rollie Fingers with the Reds leading 1–0. Fingers indicated he was going to intentionally walk Bench on a 3–2 count. As Bench prepared to go to first base, Fingers threw a pitch on the outside corner to strike him out.

9. GEORGE FRAZIER

In the 1981 World Series, New York Yankees' George Frazier became the first pitcher to lose three games in a Fall Classic. On August 3, 1982, Frazier was on the mound with the Yankees trailing the White Sox 14–2. Owner George Steinbrenner ordered the public address announcer to apologize for the Yankees' performance and offer the fans a free ticket to a future game. Humiliated, Frazier hung his head on the mound.

10. JOE DIMAGGIO

Even the greats have their humbling moments. Toward the end of his career, the Yankees' Joe DiMaggio got involved in a feud with manager Casey Stengel. On July 8, 1951, DiMaggio made an error and was replaced in the second inning by rookie Jackie Jensen. DiMaggio retired at the end of the 1951 season.

Unlikely World Series Heroes

The World Series is a separate entity from the regular season. Everything is magnified; a clutch hit of an error has more significance than in a regular season game. One good play or a key hit can transform an ordinary player into a hero. Cleveland's Bill Wambsganss made an unassisted triple play in the 1920 World Series. Four years later, rookie Washington outfielder Earl McNeely became a hero when his ground ball hit a pebble and bounced over Fred Lindstrom's head for the series' winning hit. In 1983 light-hitting Baltimore catcher Rick Dempsey was named the World Series' Most Valuable Player after batting .385. Here are some of baseball's unexpected Mr. Octobers.

1. DON LARSEN

Pitcher Don Larsen had a 3–21 record with Baltimore in 1954. Larsen had the reputation of a man

who enjoyed the nightlife. His manager in Baltimore, Jimmy Dykes, said, "The only thing he fears
is sleep."

A month before the 1956 World Series, Larsen
adopted his distinctive no-windup delivery. Larsen
started Game two of the 1956 Series and was
knocked out of the box in the third inning of a
13–8 loss to Brooklyn. Expectations weren't high
three days later when Larsen started Game five.
Larsen pitched the only perfect game in World
Series history as the Yankees won 2–0.

2. BILL BEVENS

Pitcher Bill Bevens was only 7–13 for the Yankees
in 1947. In Game four of the 1947 World Series, he
was one out away from pitching a no-hitter when
Dodgers' pinch hitter Cookie Lavagetto hit a double to drive in the winning runs as Brooklyn defeated New York 3–2. Neither Bevins nor Lavagetto
played another game in the major leagues.

3. AL GIONFRIDDO

Al Gionfriddo batted only .175 and was used
mainly as a defensive replacement by Brooklyn in
1947. During Game six of the 1947 World Series,
Gionfriddo made a sensational catch of a 415-
foot drive by New York's Joe DiMaggio, causing
the Yankee Clipper to kick the dirt in disgust. Like

Bevins and Lavagetto, Gionfriddo never played in another major league game.

4. NIPPY JONES

First baseman Nippy Jones had not played in the major leagues for five seasons when he joined the Milwaukee Braves in 1957. Used sparingly, he was sent up as a pinch hitter in the fourth game of the 1957 World Series against New York. Jones insisted that he had been hit on the foot by a pitch thrown by Tommy Byrne. Braves' manager Fred Haney pointed out to umpire Augie Donatelli that there was shoe polish on the ball. Jones was awarded first base, and the Braves rallied to win the game and the series.

5. DUSTY RHODES

Dusty Rhodes, a .253 career hitter, outhit teammate Willie Mays in the 1954 World Series. Rhodes batted .667 with seven RBIs, including a game-winning three-run home run in Game one. Rhodes's heroics helped his New York Giants sweep the heavily favored Cleveland Indians, winners of a record 111 games, in four games.

6. SANDY AMOROS

Brooklyn outfielder Sandy Amoros entered Game seven of the 1956 World Series as a defensive replacement. The move paid off immediately as Amoros made a sensational running catch to rob the Yankees' Yogi Berra of an extra base hit. Amoros's game-saving catch propelled the Brooklyn Dodgers to a 2–0 victory and their only world championship.

7. BRIAN DOYLE

During his four-year career, second baseman Brian Doyle batted a feeble .161. The unlikely batting star of the 1978 World Series, Doyle batted .438 and scored four runs. His play helped the New York Yankees defeat the Los Angeles Dodgers in six games.

8. CHUCK ESSEGIAN

Rarely used outfielder Chuck Essegian hit two pinch hit home runs during the 1959 World Series. His homers in Game two and Game six helped the Los Angeles Dodgers defeat the Chicago White Sox in six games.

9. AL WEIS

Al Weis had a .219 career average, but his timely hitting was one of the main reasons the Miracle Mets upset the Baltimore Orioles in the 1969 World Series. Weis drove in the winning run in Game two, then hit a game-tying home run in Game five. For the series, Weis batted .455.

10. **BILLY HATCHER**

Cincinnati Reds' outfielder Billy Hatcher set a World Series record when he collected seven hits in his first seven at-bats during the 1990 Fall Classic against Oakland. Hatcher batted .750 as the Reds swept the heavily favored A's in four games.

Goats

A goat is a player who loses a big game because of a crucial mistake. It may be a base-running blunder, a muffed fly ball, or an ill-timed gopher ball. More often than not, the goat is a star player. Oakland A's relief ace Dennis Eckersley gave up Kirk Gibson's dramatic home run in the 1988 World Series. Former Triple Crown winner Heinie Zimmerman chased Eddie Collins across home plate in the 1917 World Series. Many of these players had excellent careers marred by one boneheaded play.

1. RALPH BRANCA

From 1947 until 1951, Ralph Branca was one of the aces of the Brooklyn Dodgers staff. He won twenty-one games in 1947. Intelligent and personable, he didn't deserve the fate that awaited him.

Branca's Dodgers blew a thirteen-game lead in the final two months of the 1951 season and faced the New York Giants in a best-of-three play-off for the National League pennant. Branca had lost a game in the 1946 playoffs against St. Louis, but he was selected to start Game one against the Giants even though he had been beaten by New York six times during the season. He lost the first game 3–1 on a two-run home run by Bobby Thomson. The Dodgers easily won Game two, setting the stage for the deciding Game three. With twenty-game winner Don Newcombe on the mound for Brooklyn, the Dodgers led 4–2 in the ninth inning. There were two out and two runners on base when Ralph Branca was brought in to face Bobby Thomson. On a 0–1 pitch, Thomson hit a Branca high fastball over the left field fence for a game-winning home run. The "Shot Heard Round the World" gave the Giants the pennant and made Ralph Branca the goat. A photograph of Branca lying face down on the clubhouse steps symbolized his frustration.

2. BILL BUCKNER

Bill Buckner had over 2,700 hits during his career and won the National League batting crown in 1980. However, he will be forever remembered as the man who booted Mookie Wilson's grounder in the sixth game of the 1986 World Series. The Boston Red Sox had taken a 5–3 lead in the tenth inning and needed only one more out to clinch their first world championship in nearly seventy years. An improbable rally by the Mets tied the score. When Mookie Wilson's grounder went through Buckner's legs, the Mets tied the series. Two nights later, New York defeated Boston 8–5 to win the series. Buckner moved from Boston to Idaho and was traded the next season.

In Buckner's defense, his mobility was limited by bad ankles that had plagued him throughout the year. All season, manager John McNamara had been taking Buckner out in the late innings for a defensive replacement. Reliever Calvin Schiraldi deserves his share of blame. He was on the mound when the Mets rallied in Game six, and he was 0–2 in the series with a 13.50 earned run average.

3. FRED MERKLE

Fred "Bonehead" Merkle is that rare goat who made his historic blunder in the regular season. The New York Giants and Chicago Cubs were locked in a tight pennant race in 1908. On September 23, the Giants and Cubs were tied in the bottom of the ninth when Al Bridwell hit what appeared to be a game-winning single. Nineteen-year-old rookie Fred Merkle was the runner on first base. As the winning run scored, Merkle ran into the clubhouse without bothering to touch second. Chicago's Johnny Evers got the ball and stepped on second base, and the umpire called Merkle out. Since the game couldn't be resumed because the crowd had spilled out onto the field, National League president Harry Pulliam ruled that the game should be replayed only if necessary to decide the pennant. As it turned out, the teams ended up tied at the end of the regular season. When the Cubs won the playoff, Merkle's status as baseball's first great goat was ensured.

4. MITCH WILLIAMS

Mitch "Wild Thing" Williams saved forty-three games during the 1993 season for the Philadelphia Phillies. In Game four of the 1993 World Series against Toronto, the Phillies led 14–9 in the eighth inning and seemed certain to tie the series at two games apiece. The "Wild Thing" entered the game, and Toronto rallied for six runs and a 15–14 come-from-behind win. After the Phillies won Game five, Williams had a chance to redeem himself. The Phillies were leading 6–5 in the ninth inning when Williams surrendered a series-winning three-run homer to the Blue Jays' Joe Carter. Williams was 0–2 in the series with a 20.25 earned run average. After receiving numerous death threats from rabid Philadelphia fans, Williams was traded to Houston.

5. MICKEY OWEN

Mickey Owen was a solid defensive catcher who set a National League record by handling 476 chances without an error. In Game four of the 1941 World Series, Owen's Dodgers were leading the Yankees 4–3 in the ninth inning. With two out, pitcher Hugh Casey struck out Tommy Heinrich for the apparent game-winning out. Owen let the ball go to the backstop, allowing Heinrich to reach base. Owen's passed ball opened up the floodgates, and New York rallied for a 7–4 victory. The next day the Yankees won the series. It's probably unfair to single out Owen's miscue as the cause of the Dodgers' demise. He didn't give up the four runs in the ninth. It's also likely that Casey's pitch that got by Owen was a spitball, which is difficult to catch because of its sudden drop. Since the Yankees won the series in five games, they probably would have won anyway.

6. CHARLIE LEIBRANDT

For most of his career Charlie Leibrandt was a dependable lefthanded starter for Kansas City and Atlanta. In the sixth game of the 1991 World Series against Minnesota, his eleventh inning gopher ball to Kirby Puckett cost Atlanta the game in a series they went on to lose. A year later, Leibrandt gave up a two-run double to Toronto's Dave Winfield that helped clinch the world championship for the Blue Jays.

7. TOM NIEDENFUER

One of baseball's most underrated goats was Dodgers' pitcher Tom Niedenfuer. The hard-throwing reliever had fanned 102 in 106 innings during the 1985 season. In Game five of the 1985 National League championship series between Los Angeles and St. Louis, Niedenfuer gave up a game-winning home run to shortstop Ozzie Smith, his first ever from the left side of the plate. The next game Niedenfuer surrendered a towering game-winning home run to Jack Clark that sent St. Louis to the World Series.

8. WILLIE DAVIS

Willie Davis had over 2,500 base hits in his eighteen-year career and was a fleet outfielder. His difficulties during the 1966 World Series helped Baltimore sweep Los Angeles in four games. During the fifth inning of Game two, Davis made three errors as Jim Palmer defeated Sandy Koufax 6–0. Davis was in good company as the

Willie Davis
Los Angeles outfielder Willie Davis made
three costly errors during Game two of
the 1966 World Series.

Dodgers made six errors in the game. Los
Angeles was shut out the final three games and
hit only .142 for the series. Davis was even worse,
with only one hit and a .063 batting average.

9. ROGER PECKINPAUGH

Washington shortstop Roger Peckinpaugh had
been one of the heroes of the 1924 World Series,
with a game-winning double in Game two and a
.417 average. He was voted the American League
Most Valuable Player in 1925, largely because of
his defensive prowess. During the 1925 World

Series against Pittsburgh, his eight errors, including two costly miscues in the seventh and deciding game, doomed the Senators.

10. **FRED SNODGRASS**

Fred Snodgrass is almost as famous a goat as teammate Fred Merkel. His claim to shame occurred in the tenth inning of the eighth and final game of the 1912 World Series against Boston. Snodgrass dropped Clyde Engel's fly ball for a two-base error. Even though he made a sensational game-saving catch (which he called the best of his career) to rob Harry Hooper, Snodgrass received the blame when Boston rallied to win the game 3–2.

Spoilers and Nemeses

There are players whose notoriety comes at the expense of other players or teams. In 1908 Chicago pitcher Ed Reulbach defeated the Dodgers a record nine times. Ripper Collins called himself the "All-American Louse" because he broke up four no-hitters.

1. HUB "SCHUCKS" PRUETT

Hub Pruett had an undistinguished career, winning twenty-nine and losing forty-eight. It seemed that the only batter the screwball-throwing southpaw could get out consistently was Babe Ruth. During his rookie season in 1922, Shucks fanned Ruth thirteen times in sixteen at-bats.

2. LARRY JASTER

No pitcher has ever dominated a team in a year like Cardinals' lefthander Larry Jaster did the

Dodgers in 1966. In five starts, Jaster shut out the pennant winners five times. He held Los Angeles to twenty-four singles in those appearances.

3. FRANK LARY

Detroit pitcher Frank Lary won twenty-one games in 1956 and twenty-three in 1961. He was known as the "Yankee Killer" for good reason. Lary was 7–0 against the Bronx Bombers in 1958 and defeated them five times in a row in 1959. Overall, Lary was 27–13 against New York.

4. CESAR TOVAR

On September 22, 1968, Cesar Tovar of the Minnesota Twins played every position in a game against Oakland. The versatile Tovar led the American League at various times in hits, doubles, and triples. Tovar was the ultimate spoiler, breaking up five no-hitters during his career. The pitchers victimized by Tovar were Barry Moore (1967), Dave McNally (1969), Mike Cuellar (1969), Dick Bosman (1970), and Catfish Hunter (1975).

5. JIM BAGBY JR.

On July 17, 1941, pitcher Jim Bagby Jr. of the Cleveland Indians stopped Joe DiMaggio's fifty-six-game hitting streak when he induced him to hit into a double play in the eighth inning. Bagby was the son of Jim Bagby, a former thirty-game winner. In the minors DiMaggio had a sixty-one-game hitting streak stopped by Ed Walsh Jr., the son of Ed Walsh, baseball's last forty-game winner.

6. HAL GRIGGS

In 1957, Ted Williams set a record by reaching base sixteen consecutive times. He seemed like a cinch to extend the streak when he faced Washington's Hal Griggs. After all, Griggs would finish his career with a 6–26 record and a dreadful 5.50 earned run average. Somehow Griggs enticed Williams to ground out to end his streak.

7. HOWIE BEDELL

Don Drysdale's record 58⅔ consecutive shutout innings streak was broken in the fifth inning of a game against Philadelphia on June 8, 1968. The run was scored on a sacrifice fly by Howie Bedell. It was Bedell's only run batted in that season and one of only three in his career.

8. JIM QUALLS

Tom Seaver of the New York Mets was one out away from a perfect game against Chicago on July 9, 1969. The batter, Jim Qualls, was a rookie outfielder who finished his career with a .223 batting average. Qualls spoiled the perfect game with a single to left-center. Seaver did pitch a no-hitter with the Cincinnati Reds in 1978.

9. LARRY STAHL

Larry Stahl of the San Diego Padres, a .252 life-time hitter, broke up a perfect game without even taking the bat off his shoulder. On September 2, 1972, Chicago's Milt Pappas retired twenty-six consecutive batters before he walked Stahl on a 3–2 count. Pappas always insisted that the pitch was a strike, and the umpire blew the call.

10. CHUCK CHURN

Pittsburgh's Elroy Face won his first seventeen decisions in 1959. Because of wins in his last five decisions in 1958, the forkballer's twenty-two consecutive victories placed him just two short of Carl Hubbell's major league record. On September 11, 1959, Face lost a 5–4 decision to the Los Angeles Dodgers. The winning pitcher was Chuck Churn, and the victory was one of only three in his career.

What Might Have Been

Baseball can be a cruel game. On September 15, 1971, Larry Yount, a promising pitcher for Houston, was making his major league debut. He injured his shoulder on his first warm-up pitch and never pitched in a major league game. His brother, Robin, would have a brilliant career and be one of the few players to make more than 3,000 hits. All of these players had potentially great careers shortened by injury or other circumstances.

1. HERB SCORE

Cleveland southpaw Herb Score led the American League in strikeouts his first two seasons and won twenty games in 1956. He was only twenty-three years old when he faced the New York Yankees on May 7, 1957. The Yankees' Gil McDougald lined a pitch that struck Score in the face. The pitcher fell to the ground, bleeding from his nose and mouth. He suffered a broken nose and a potential loss of vision in his right eye. Score missed the remainder of the season. When he returned the following year, he was not the same pitcher. Score's record before the injury was 38–20, but 17–26 after.

2. TONY CONIGLIARO

The tragic story of Tony Conigliaro is truly one of unrealized potential. Conigliaro was only twenty when he led the American League in home runs, the youngest ever to do so. Two years later, on August 18, 1967, the Red Sox outfielder was beaned by Angels' pitcher Jack Hamilton. The pitch fractured his cheekbone, dislocated his jaw, and damaged his eyesight. Conigliaro missed the rest of the season, as well as the following year, while his vision improved. He made an amazing comeback, and in 1970, Conigliaro belted thirty-six home runs, but deteriorating vision forced his retirement in 1975. Conigliaro suffered a debilitating heart attack in 1982 and died in 1990 at the age of forty-five.

3. PETE REISER

Leo Durocher observed that Pete Reiser may have been the best ball player he ever saw. "He had everything but luck," said Leo the Lip. In 1941, the twenty-two-year-old Brooklyn outfielder won the

batting title and led the National League in doubles, triples, runs scored, and slugging percentage
despite two serious beanings. Reiser was batting
.383 on July 2, 1942, when he suffered a fractured skull from crashing into the outfield wall in
St. Louis. After three years of relative safety in the
military service during World War II, Reiser resumed his stay on the disabled list by breaking
his ankle sliding into a base in 1946. The following year Reiser ran into the Ebbets Field wall with
such force that he was given last rites. It was one
of eleven times that Reiser was carried off the
field. Seven times he either broke his collarbone
or dislocated his shoulder. Other injuries included
a broken neck, temporary paralysis, and a blood
clot on the brain.

4. **J. R. RICHARD**

At 6 feet 8 inches, J. R. Richard intimidated hitters in much the same way that Randy Johnson
does today. Richard struck out fifteen batters in
his first major league game in 1971, but it would
be another five years before he became a consis-
tent winner. Richard won twenty games in 1976
and struck out over 300 batters in both 1978 and
1979. On July 30, 1980, Richard, who had been
complaining of impaired vision and sluggishness,
collapsed. A stroke had paralyzed his left side.

Although his condition did improve gradually, his comeback attempts were unsuccessful.

5. **RAY FOSSE**

Ray Fosse was the best young catcher in the American League when he was bowled over by Pete Rose in a home plate collision at the 1970 All-Star Game. The twenty-three-year-old catcher suffered a fractured shoulder and never displayed the potential he had exhibited prior to the injury. He had several stints on the disabled list. Fosse pinched a nerve in his neck trying to break up a fight in the clubhouse, and his foot was injured by a cherry bomb thrown by a fan. By 1975 his batting average had slipped to .140.

6. **AUSTIN MCHENRY**

St. Louis outfielder Austin McHenry was on his way to stardom in 1921 when he batted .350, with 201 hits and 102 runs batted in. Midway through the next season it was discovered that he had a brain tumor. McHenry died on November 27, 1922 at the age of twenty-seven.

7. **DAVE ORR**

Dave Orr was one of the great hitters of the 1880s. Never hitting below .300, Orr compiled a .342 career batting average. At 5 feet 11 inches,

250 pounds, he was an imposing sight. In 1893, he had his greatest season, batting .373 for Brooklyn. Orr was only thirty-one years old when a stroke ended his career.

8. BILL "LITTLE EVA" LANGE

Bill "Little Eva" Lange was such a great baserunner and hitter that he has been compared to Ty Cobb. Lange once held out in order that he could attend a heavyweight title fight featuring Gentleman Jim Corbett. A .330 lifetime hitter, he retired in 1899 at age twenty-eight to marry the daughter of a real estate magnate. His father-in-law disapproved of his daughter marrying a baseball player.

9. VON MCDANIEL

Eighteen-year-old Von McDaniel pitched a two-hit shutout against the Dodgers in his first major league start on June 4, 1957. A month later, the Cardinals' righthander threw a one-hitter against Pittsburgh. The next spring McDaniel injured his shoulder and pitched only two more innings in the majors. While Von McDaniel was finished at age nineteen, his brother Lindy pitched in the majors for twenty-one years.

10. WAYNE SIMPSON

Rookie pitcher Wayne Simpson was a principal reason that the 1970 Cincinnati Reds won 70 of their first 100 games. The twenty-one-year-old righthander won thirteen of his first fourteen decisions, including a one-hitter and a two-hitter. Selected to the All-Star Game, Simpson injured his shoulder and won only one more game that season. For the remainder of his career, Simpson had a record of 22–28.

Blackballed

On August 28, 1945, Jackie Robinson signed a contract to play professional baseball for the Montreal Royals, a farm club of the Brooklyn Dodgers. The signing was not announced publicly until October 23. Jackie Robinson broke baseball's color barrier with Brooklyn in 1947. In fact, many African Americans had paved the way for Robinson's breakthrough.

1. FLEET WALKER

Moses Fleetwood Walker actually played major league baseball sixty-three years before Jackie Robinson's first game. In 1884 Fleet Walker played in forty-two games for the Toledo Blue Stockings of the American Association, then considered a major league. Walker soon realized that he was a marked man. The catcher developed a primitive form of wooden shin guard to protect his legs from the well-aimed spikes of opposing baserunners. Even his teammates attempted to hurt Walker. Pitcher Tony Mullane threw the ball in the dirt, hoping to injure him. Mullane refused to take Walker's signals, but grudgingly admitted, "He was the best catcher I ever worked with." During the season Walker was attacked by a mob of abusive fans in Louisville. When blacks were banned from the major leagues, he played for several years in the minors.

An educated man, Walker attended Oberlin College and the University of Michigan. In 1891, he stabbed a man who had attacked him and was acquitted by an all-white jury. In 1908, Walker wrote a booklet on race in America entitled *Our Home Colony* in which he suggested that blacks could never achieve equality in America, and the best solution would be for them to return to Africa. During his last years Walker was editor of a newspaper, *The Steubenville Equator,* and owned several movie theaters.

2. WELDAY WALKER

Fleet Walker's younger brother, Welday, played five games in the outfield for Toledo in 1884. After African Americans were blacklisted from professional baseball, Welday filed a protest, reasoning that ability, not color, should determine whether a player be permitted to play on a team.

3. SANDY NAVA

Dark-skinned catcher Sandy Nava passed himself off as a Spaniard, Mexican, and even an Italian. Nava (whose real name was Irwin Sandy) carried off the ruse successfully enough to remain in the American Association until 1886. Nava has the distinction of being the first man of color to play in the National League, having played with Providence from 1882 to 1884.

4. GEORGE TREADWAY

Outfielder George Treadway claimed American Indian ancestry and was permitted to play in the major leagues until 1896. His best season was 1894 when he batted .328 and drove in 102 runs for Brooklyn.

5. GEORGE STOVEY

George Stovey, a light-skinned black from Canada, won a record thirty-five games for Newark of the Eastern League in 1887. That year, John Montgomery Ward, captain of the New York Giants, attempted to sign Stovey, but was blocked by the protests of Chicago's Cap Anson and others.

6. CHARLIE GRANT

In 1901, John McGraw, the manager of the American League Baltimore Orioles, was in Hot Springs, Arkansas, for spring training and there discovered a black bellhop named Charlie Grant. He was such a good second baseman that McGraw wanted to sign him. McGraw devised a plan in which he would attempt to pass off Grant as Chief Tokohoma, a full-blooded Cherokee. The plan was foiled by owner Charles Comiskey, who exposed Grant's true identity.

7. FRANK GRANT

Second baseman Frank Grant may have been the most talented African American player of the nineteenth century. Compared favorably to the white stars in the major leagues, Grant batted as high as .366 and won the International League batting title in 1877. His Buffalo teammates refused to sit with him for a team portrait, and Grant once had to grab a club to escape a beating. In Toronto, he endured chants of "Kill the nigger." Even more painful was the racism that kept him from playing in the major leagues.

8. RAMON HERRARA

Ramon Herrara, a Cuban infielder, played in the American League with Boston in 1925 and 1926.

Herrara holds the distinction of playing in both the major leagues and Negro Leagues.

9. BUD FOWLER

Bud Fowler broke professional baseball's color line when he played for New Castle in 1872. A superb pitcher and second baseman, Fowler played in numerous minor leagues, usually batting above .300. Had he not been black, he surely would have had the opportunity to play in the major leagues.

10. CHET BREWER

Chet Brewer nearly became the man who broke the color barrier. In 1943, Oakland owner Vince De Vicenzi wanted to give Brewer a tryout, but his manager, Johnny Vergez, refused. Two years later, Bakersfield, a farm team of the Cleveland Indians, wanted to give Brewer a tryout, but the plan was nixed by the parent team. Brewer, an outstanding pitcher, once won thirty games in the Negro League and pitched two no-hitters in the Mexican League.

Racism in Baseball

It seems almost unbelievable that blacks were not permitted to play in the major leagues until 1947. Since its beginnings, however, major league baseball has been plagued by racism. Ty Cobb refused to room with Babe Ruth because it was rumored he had African ancestry. Pitcher Kirby Higbe boasted that he had strengthened his arm by throwing rocks at blacks as a child in South Carolina. The following incidents represent the dark side of our national pastime.

1. CAP ANSON

Cap Anson was the dominant player of the nineteenth century. His tremendous influence on the game was instrumental in the establishment of the color barrier. In 1884, Chicago, managed by Anson, was scheduled to play an exhibition game against Toledo. When he saw their black catcher,

Fleet Walker, he yelled, "Get that nigger off the field." Toledo's manager insisted that Walker play, and Anson relented. Three years later, Anson again refused to play an exhibition game against a minor league team with black players. That same day, owners agreed to institute a color line. African Americans were not allowed to play in the major leagues for another sixty years.

2. KENESAW MOUNTAIN LANDIS

Considered the savior of baseball after he helped restore the game's integrity following the Black Sox scandal, baseball commissioner Kenesaw Mountain Landis must bear much of the responsibility for maintaining baseball's color barrier. Landis insisted that there was no formal rule that banned blacks from playing professional baseball. Despite his assurances, Landis blocked Washington and Pittsburgh from signing black players in the early 1940s. When Bill Veeck attempted to buy the Philadelphia Phillies in 1943 and stock the team with black players, Landis made sure another owner was found. A year after Landis's death, Branch Rickey signed Jackie Robinson.

3. JAKE POWELL

New York outfielder Jake Powell shocked radio audiences during an interview in Chicago on July 29, 1938. A policeman in the offseason, Powell

told interviewer Bob Elson that he derived plea-
sure from "cracking niggers over the head." Commissioner Landis suspended Powell for ten days
for the racist remark. He was forced to apologize
only after leaders of the African American commu-
nity threatened to organize a boycott of Yankees'
owner Jacob Ruppert's brewery products. In 1948,
Powell committed suicide in a Washington, D. C.,
police station after being questioned about a bad
check charge.

4. BEN CHAPMAN

Another former Yankee outfielder, Ben Chapman
reflected the racism that Jackie Robinson encoun-
tered when he joined the Brooklyn Dodgers in
1947. Chapman, the manager of the Philadelphia
Phillies, baited Robinson with a steady stream of
racial taunts. His insults compared blacks with
monkeys and implied that they were thick-skulled
and contracted venereal diseases. Chapman and
some of his players would aim their bats at Robinson and make machine-gun sounds. Chapman
was fired as Phillies' skipper in 1948.

5. DIXIE WALKER

Some of Jackie Robinson's worst opposition ini-
tially came from his Brooklyn teammates. Dixie
Walker, the 1944 National League batting champion, circulated a petition objecting to Robinson's

promotion to the big league club. The petition was ignored by manager Leo Durocher, and Walker demanded to be traded. The Georgia native came to accept playing with Robinson, but he was traded to Pittsburgh at season's end.

6. CLAY HOPPER

Jackie Robinson faced prejudice in the minors while playing for Montreal. His manager, the Mississippi-born Clay Hopper, reportedly asked Branch Rickey, "Do you really think a nigger is a human being?"

7. GEORGE WEISS

During his twenty-nine seasons (1932–60) with the New York Yankees, executive George Weiss oversaw teams that won nineteen pennants and fifteen world championships. Weiss expressed his reluctance to integrate the Yankees when he admitted, "I will never allow a black man to wear a Yankees uniform." Eight years after Jackie Robinson broke the color barrier, the Yankees finally brought up a black player, Elston Howard. Manager Casey Stengel marked the occasion by saying, "When I finally get a nigger, I get the only one who can't run."

8. TOM YAWKEY

The New York Yankees were positively progressive in race relations compared to the Boston Red Sox. The Red Sox, owned by Tom Yawkey, were the last major league team to integrate. The first black, Pumpsie Green, did not join the Red Sox until 1959.

9. HANK AARON

In 1974, Hank Aaron was about to surpass Babe Ruth's career home run record. What should have been one of the happiest moments of Aaron's life became a nightmare. During his quest for the record, the Atlanta Braves' outfielder received many racist threats. There was even a plot to kidnap his daughter, Gaile. He received police protection and took seriously the numerous death threats he received. "It was hell," Aaron remembered. It was no way to treat a hero.

10. AL CAMPANIS

While blacks had gained acceptance as players, progress in the positions of manager and executives has been slow. On April 6, 1987, Los Angeles Dodgers' General Manager Al Campanis appeared on *Nightline* on the occasion of the fortieth anniversary of Jackie Robinson's debut in the majors. Campanis outraged many when he suggested that African Americans "lacked some of the necessities" to become managers and hold front office positions. As the result of his remarks, Campanis was fired, and major league baseball hired more blacks in executive and managerial positions.

Kill the Umpire

"Kill the umpire" is more than just a baseball adage. Here are some frightening examples where the men in blue became black and blue.

1. SAMUEL WHITE

Minor league umpire Samuel White was hit over the head and killed during a game in Alabama in 1899.

2. ORA JENNINGS

In 1901, another minor league umpire, Ora Jennings, met the same fate during a game in Indiana.

3. HANK O'DAY

Hank O'Day was a National League umpire from 1893 until 1927. Early in his career, O'Day was badly beaten by irate St. Louis Cardinal fans after a disputed call. Armed police escorted the besieged umpire down the street, where he was pelted with rocks.

4. BILLY EVANS

Umpire Billy Evans had his skull fractured when he was struck in the head by a bottle thrown by a fan during a game at Sportsman's Park in 1907. In 1921, the umpire was attacked by Ty Cobb underneath the stadium in Washington, D. C. Cobb repeatedly smashed Evans's head into the concrete wall.

5. JACK WARNER

New York Giants' catcher Jack Warner was suspended five days for striking an umpire in 1903. Two days later, he was used as a substitute umpire when the men in blue didn't show up.

6. WILLIAM "LORD" BYRON

Baseball's original singing umpire, William "Lord" Byron, has the distinction of being punched out by both John McGraw and Ty Cobb. Byron, who sometimes sang out his calls, was an umpire in the major leagues from 1913 to 1919. On another occasion, he was chased from the field by a mob of angry rock-wielding fans.

7. SHERRY MAGEE

Sherry Magee was an outfielder who played between 1904 and 1910 and led the National League in runs batted in four times. While playing for Philadelphia, he broke the umpire's jaw after arguing a called third strike. Magee became an umpire himself in 1928.

8. BILLY MCLEAN

In 1906, Billy McLean was a twenty-two-year-old rookie umpire when he had his skull fractured by a flying bottle. Later in his career he was arrested after injuring a heckling fan by throwing a bat into the stands.

9. GEORGE MAGERKURTH

Before becoming an umpire, burly George Magerkurth had fought in seventy professional fights. His pugilistic training became useful in the minor leagues when he fought a promising first baseman named Ivy Griffin. Griffin took such a beating that it ended his career. In 1939, Giants' shortstop Billy Jurges got into a fight with Magerkurth after he claimed the umpire spit tobacco juice in his face. The following year a man out on parole attacked Magerkurth during a game at Ebbets Field. Magerkurth's lowest moment came in 1945 when he beat up a fan in Cincinnati who he thought was heckling him. The victim turned out to be a Dayton restaurant owner who was seated near the real culprit.

10. **TIM HURST**

Tim Hurst has the dubious honor of being the only umpire to be thrown out of both the National and American Leagues. Hurst kept players in line by hitting them over the head with his mask or by pinching them hard. In 1897, Hurst was barred from the National League for hitting a fan in Cincinnati with a beer stein. Twelve years later, he was given the heave-ho by the American League for spitting in the face of second baseman Eddie Collins.

Media Blitz

Infielder Rocky Bridges said, "I know what the word 'media' means. It's plural for mediocre." The relationship between ballplayers and the media has never been especially cordial. For years Steve Carlton refused to speak to the press. Albert Belle was accused of throwing a ball at a journalist. Here are examples of instances where the reporters made the headlines.

1. BILLY MARTIN

Billy Martin's unique rapport with players carried over to his relationships with the media. In 1978, Billy punched *Nevada State Journal* writer Ray Hager. Martin also called reporters Henry Hecht a "prick" and Deborah Herschel a "hooker."

2. PATSY TEBEAU

Henry Chadwick wrote that Cleveland manager Patsy Tebeau degraded the game of baseball more

Ted Williams
One of baseball's greatest hitters, Ted Williams
had a less than cordial relationship with the
media.

than any other player. Tebeau repeatedly assaulted
umpires and once tore up a horseshoe wreath of
flowers given to player Cupid Childs on a day
honoring him. In 1896, Patsy beat up Cleveland reporter Elmer Pasco for negative remarks he made
about Tebeau's Spiders.

3. BRET SABERHAGEN
In 1985, Kansas City's Bret Saberhagen became
the youngest pitcher to win the Cy Young Award.

When Saberhagen was traded to the Mets, his relationship with the New York media was less than cordial. He sprayed a container of bleach on reporters, an offense that resulted in a five-game suspension. Earlier in the season Saberhagen tossed a firecracker into a crowd of reporters.

4. DAVE KINGMAN

Slugger Dave Kingman once showed his displeasure with a sportswriter by throwing a ten-gallon bucket of icewater over his head. He went too far when he sent a rat to a female reporter at the *Sacramento Bee.* Despite hitting thirty-five home runs for the Oakland A's in 1986, he was not offered a contract, costing him a chance to hit 500 home runs.

5. TED WILLIAMS

Ted Williams may have spit at fans in Boston, but he really hated the media. Teddy Ballgame was known to reply to interview requests by replying, "Go fuck off." If a writer approached him, the Splendid Splinter might remark, "Hey, what stinks? It was the shit you wrote last night." Thumper once lifted *Boston Globe* writer Hy Hurwitz up by his necktie, then cut the tie with scissors.

6. **DEION SANDERS**

In 1992, Deion Sanders attempted to become the first athlete to play in a professional baseball and football game on the same day. During the afternoon Deion played cornerback for the Atlanta Falcons. That night, he suited up to play outfield for the Atlanta Braves in the National League championship series against Pittsburgh. When he was criticized by CBS announcer Tim McCarver for risking injury by playing in an NFL game on the day of a crucial baseball playoff game, Sanders doused him three times with icewater in the clubhouse.

7. **DENNY MCLAIN**

Denny McLain won thirty-one games with the 1968 Detroit Tigers, but his world fell apart a few years later. In April 1970, he was suspended for his involvement in a bookmaking operation and in September of that same year for possession of a gun. In between, he dumped icewater on two Detroit sportswriters after a game.

8. **GEORGE BRETT**

Kansas City third baseman George Brett batted .390 in 1980 and was the American League's Most Valuable Player. Rather than reporting on his on-field achievements, Brett felt that the media concentrated too much on his problem with hemorrhoids. Brett reportedly once shoved a woman reporter and swung a crutch at another.

9. JIM KERN

Jim Kern pitched in the major leagues from 1974 to 1986. The flaky pitcher once ate the notes of a sportswriter after being told he might have to eat his words. On a airplane he once ate the pages of a book that a reporter was reading.

10. JOHN MCGRAW

John McGraw battled umpires, players, and reporters. In 1905, Little Napoleon cursed at a reporter, then grabbed his nose and twisted it.

Fanatics

I n the nineteenth century, spectators were called kranks. St. Louis owner Chris Von der Ahe referred to them as fanatics, which was shortened to fans. Throughout the history of baseball, some fans have acted like fanatics. In 1991, San Francisco pitcher Steve Decker sprained his left foot running from a horde of autograph hounds. The year before he broke Babe Ruth's single season home run record, Roger Maris was nearly struck by jagged pieces of grandstand seats thrown by Detroit fans. When fans cross the line, no one is safe.

1. EDDIE WAITKUS

Eddie Waitkus played first base for the Chicago Cubs in the late 1940s. While Waitkus was with the Cubs, a teenage girl named Ruth Ann Steinhagen became infatuated with him. She kept a shrine to him at the foot of her bed. Steinhagen was disconsolate when Waitkus was traded to Philadelphia after the 1948 season. She decided that if she couldn't have him, no one would. During a road trip to Chicago, Steinhagen arranged for a meeting in a room at the Edgewater Beach Hotel. Steinhagen told him, "I have a surprise for you." She pulled a rifle from the closet and shot Waitkus in the chest. Instead of finishing him off with a knife and killing herself, as she planned, Steinhagen briefly held his hand and then notified the front desk. Waitkus recovered and had his best season in 1950, helping the Whiz Kids to the pennant. Steinhagen spent three years in a mental hospital. She later claimed that the shooting had relieved her tension and that she had never felt so happy.

2. **1895 CLEVELAND SPIDERS**

The 1895 Temple Cup between the Baltimore Orioles and Cleveland Spiders was marred by several ugly incidents. During Game one in Cleveland, fans threw vegetables at the Baltimore players. When the Spiders defeated the Orioles in Baltimore, angry fans chased them from the field. The Spiders were paraded through the streets of Baltimore where they were stoned by irate fans.

3. **1908 CHICAGO CUBS**

The Chicago Cubs and New York Giants met in a one-game playoff to decide the National League champion of 1908. The Cubs, behind the pitching of Three Finger Brown, defeated the Giants and Christy Mathewson 4–2. Giants' fans knocked down the fence and drove the Chicago players from the field. The Cubs were trapped in the clubhouse for three hours before order was restored. Rioting after the game resulted in one death and extensive damage.

4. **BIRDIE TEBBETTS**

Cleveland fans were in an angry mood on September 27, 1940, when the Detroit Tigers clinched the pennant by defeating the Indians 2–0. Throughout the game the Tigers were pelted with eggs, fruits, and vegetables. The barrage culminated when Detroit bullpen catcher Birdie Tebbetts was hit with a crate of green tomatoes thrown from the stands. Umpire George Pipgras thought Tebbetts might be dead. After Tebbetts came to in the clubhouse, the police brought him the culprit. The fan was roughed up, and Tebbetts was later acquitted of assault charges.

5. WIN MERCER

Pitcher Win Mercer, a twenty-five-game winner in 1896, was the most popular player in Washington. In 1897, thousands of women came to the ballpark on Ladies Day to see their favorite. The ladies went crazy when umpire Bill Carpenter ejected Mercer during an argument. Hundreds of Mercer's female fans stormed the field and beat the beleaguered umpire to the ground. As he fled for his life, the rampaging women nearly laid waste to the ballpark before the police were summoned.

6. ROBERT JOYCE

On July 12, 1938, avid Brooklyn Dodgers' fan Robert Joyce shot and killed two men at Pat Diamond's Bar. The murders occurred following an argument with a New York Giants' fan over baseball.

7. 1984 DETROIT TIGERS

The celebration turned violent following the Detroit Tigers' victory over the San Diego Padres in Game five of the 1984 World Series. Fans rioted in the streets, torching police cars and throwing beer bottles. One person was killed, and scores were injured.

8. **WALLY JOYNER**

California first baseman Wally Joyner batted in 100 runs during his rookie season in 1986. That year he was nearly killed when he was grazed by a butcher knife thrown from the upper deck of New York's Yankee Stadium.

9. **BOB WATSON**

Houston outfielder Bob Watson was injured when he crashed into the wall at Cincinnati's Riverfront Stadium during a game against the Reds in 1974. As Watson lay bleeding on the warning track, fans showed their concern by pouring beer on the fallen player.

10. **WHITEY WITT**

On September 16, 1922, New York Yankees' centerfielder Whitey Witt was knocked unconscious by a bottle thrown from the stands at St. Louis' Sportsman's Park. The American League downplayed the incident, concocting a ludicrous scenario that Witt stepped on the bottle, which then flew up and conked him in the head.

With Teammates like These

Sometimes your teammates can be your worst enemies. Consider the following examples.

1. FRANK WARFIELD

Oliver "Ghost" Marcelle, the great Negro League third baseman, was playing winter ball in Cuba in 1928 when he got into a fight with teammate Frank Warfield. During the struggle, Warfield bit off Marcelle's nose. Marcelle wore a black patch over the hole but was so ashamed that he retired rather than show his face.

2. HEINIE ZIMMERMAN

Heinie Zimmerman won the Triple Crown in 1912 but was the goat of the 1917 World Series and was later banned from baseball for conspiring to throw games. Zimmerman nearly blinded Chicago teammate Jimmy Sheckard when he threw a bottle of ammonia at him. Manager Frank Chance grabbed Zimmerman and beat him senseless.

3. DUCKY MEDWICK

Joe "Ducky" Medwick personified the rowdy behavior of the Gas House Gang. The St. Louis outfielder terrorized opposing pitchers at the plate and his own pitchers on the field. In 1933, Cardinals' pitcher Tex Carleton was taking swings in batting practice when Medwick told him to get out of the cage and let the regulars hit. When Carleton took an extra swing, Ducky knocked him cold. Manager Gabby Street had to get another starter warmed up. Two years later, pitcher Ed Heusser made the mistake of accusing Medwick of not hustling in the outfield after a fly ball dropped in front of him. Ducky, never one to appreciate constructive criticism, flattened Heusser on the mound. A new pitcher had to be brought into the game.

4. LENNY RANDLE

On March 28, 1977, Texas Rangers' manager Frank Lucchesi was speaking with reporters behind the batting cage when he was brutally attacked by infielder Lenny Randle. Randle punched the fifty-year-old manager repeatedly until he was dragged off by teammates. His only explanation for the assault was that Lucchesi had called him a punk. Lucchesi suffered a broken jaw and required plastic surgery. To add insult to injury, Lucchesi was fired in June because management felt he had lost control of his players.

5. TY COBB

Ty Cobb was almost hated as much by his Detroit teammates as he was by the opposition. Cobb punched his roommate for having the audacity to take a bath before him. He decked pitcher Ed Siever on the final day of the 1906 season after he made a disparaging remark about Cobb's play in the outfield. Not satisfied, Cobb gave him another beating at the hotel that evening. His teammates despised Cobb to such an extent that they would do anything to make him look bad. When it appeared that Nap Lajoie had beaten Cobb out for the batting title, several Detroit players sent the popular second baseman a congratulatory telegram. Cobb was so fearful that his teammates would try to kill him that he kept a loaded gun under his pillow.

6. BUCK O'BRIEN

Buck O'Brien won twenty games for Boston in 1912, then lost Game three of the 1912 World Series to New York. When he gave up five runs in the first inning of Game six, his teammates beat him up after the game. Boston won the series four games to three, but O'Brien was traded to Chicago the next season.

7. PHENOMENAL SMITH

Pitcher John Smith nicknamed himself "Phenomenal" and claimed he was so good that he didn't even need his teammates behind him. His Brooklyn teammates took offense to Smith's remarks and decided to teach him a lesson. In his first start on June 17, 1885, the Dodgers intentionally made errors so that Smith would lose the game. The Dodgers made fourteen errors, half of them by shortstop Germany Smith in a 18–5 loss. The team fined each of the players $500, but Phenomenal was released to insure team harmony. Smith never had a winning season, and the only phenomenal thing about his eight-year career was that he managed to lose thirty games in 1887.

8. ROBERT HIGGINS

Robert Higgins was a black minor league pitcher in the 1880s. His inexcusable treatment by his Syracuse teammates typified the racism prevalent in the game. Whenever Higgins pitched, his teammates intentionally made errors, and they refused to allow him to be in the team photo.

9. OSSIE VITT

One of the most unpopular managers with his players was Cleveland skipper Ossie Vitt. He irritated the players by criticizing them in the press and chewing them out on the field when they made a bad play. Players demanded that they be traded or that Vitt be fired. They did what they could to undermine him, even if it meant losing a game. The team became known as the "Crybaby Indians" and were bombarded with baby bottles and jars of baby food. Cleveland lost the 1940 pennant by a game to Detroit, and Vitt was fired.

10. JOHNNY EVERS AND JOE TINKER

The Cubs' double play combination of Tinker to Evers to Chance was immortalized in a poem written by Franklin Adams. The men were so linked in the public mind that they were inducted together in the Hall of Fame in 1946. In fact, Tinker and Evers disliked each other intensely. The cause of the ill will was a seemingly insignificant dispute over a taxi in 1905. The two men didn't speak to one another for thirty-three years.

Donnybrooks

Jesse "The Crab" Burkett hit over .400 three times. He also was ejected in both games of a doubleheader after getting into three fights. Dour Frankie Crosetti once punched baseball clown Max Patkin. Here are some players who are guaranteed to add some punch to your lineup.

1. BILLY MARTIN

The undisputed King of the Sucker Punch, Billy Martin fought friend and foe alike. Martin was a good player and an excellent manager, but his enduring fame will be as a fighter. In 1952, he fought Boston outfielder Jimmy Piersall under the stands at Fenway Park. Two days later, Piersall was sent to the minors and suffered a nervous breakdown. Martin expressed some remorse for the incident. "I was only a jump away from the guys in the white suit myself," he admitted. That same year he decked catcher Clint "Scrap Iron" Courtney, whom Satchel Paige called "the meanest man I ever met."

Billy's most infamous fight as a player occurred in 1960. Martin, playing for Cincinnati, felt Chicago pitcher Jim Brewer had thrown at him. Martin flipped his bat at the pitcher. When Brewer tried to hand him the bat, Martin sucker punched him, breaking his cheekbone. Brewer underwent two eye operations and was out for the season. When Martin learned that Brewer had sued him for a million dollars, he smirked, "How does he want it, cash or check?"

Billy's boxing record as a manager was even more impressive. He beat up the traveling secretaries of the Minnesota Twins and Texas Rangers (the latter a sixty-year-old man). Martin flattened a reporter and, in his most famous bout, gave a fat lip to a marshmallow salesman named Joseph Cooper. Twice Martin fought his pitchers. In 1969, he knocked cold his twenty-game winner in Minnesota, Dave Boswell. The pitcher came out of the battle with a black eye, chipped tooth, and twenty stitches in his face. Billy fared less well in a 1987 encounter with Yankees' pitcher Ed Whitson. Billy's injuries included a broken right arm and bruised side. It was apparent that Billy was over the hill in 1988 when he was badly beaten in a Texas topless bar. First baseman Don Mattingly uttered his boxing epitaph, "That's like beating up your grandfather."

2. ART "THE GREAT" SHIRES

Art "The Great" Shires was a hard-hitting first baseman who batted over .300 three of his four major league seasons. In 1929, while captain of the White Sox, "Whattaman" Shires beat up his manager Lena Blackburne three times. One of the disputes concerned a red felt party hat Shires wore during batting practice. Shires decided to test his pugilistic skills as a professional. He knocked "Mysterious" Dan Daly cold in twenty-one seconds and won all of his fights except a decision loss to Chicago Bears' hulking center George Trafton. Baseball Commissioner Kenesaw Mountain Landis put a stop to his boxing career when he tried to arrange a bout with Cubs' outfielder Hack Wilson.

3. JOHN MCGRAW

By all accounts, John McGraw may not have been the best fighter in the world, but he was the most persistent. On May 16, 1894, McGraw got into a fight with Boston's Tommy Tucker, and while the two men battled, the ballpark burned down around them. Three years later, he and teammate Wee Willie Keeler fought nude on the clubhouse floor. One of McGraw's infrequent victories came in 1904 when he loosened the teeth of a young boy selling lemonade. He was less successful in 1913 when Philadelphia pitcher Ad Brennan decked him. The Giants' skipper was so hated that grateful fans sent Brennan a bouquet of flowers. McGraw had many encounters with umpires; the most famous came in 1917 when he belted Lord Byron, baseball's singing umpire. One of McGraw's most humiliating defeats came in 1920 when he received two black eyes in a scuffle with actor William Boyd, who later gained fame as Hopalong Cassidy.

4. **BOSS SCHMIDT**

Ty Cobb met his match when he challenged Detroit catcher Charley "Boss" Schmidt. Schmidt could hammer nails into wood with his bare hands and had once fought an exhibition against heavyweight champion Jack Johnson. Schmidt gave Cobb a merciless beating, breaking his nose and nearly closing both eyes.

5. **DOLF CAMILLI**

First baseman Dolf Camilli batted in more than 100 runs five times between 1936 and 1942. A no-nonsense type of player, Camilli came from a boxing family. His brother had died in the ring in a bout with Max Baer, the heavyweight champion. Dolf also had professional boxing experience that he put to use when necessary. He punched out Joe Medwick when he saw him bullying young shortstop Pee Wee Reese.

6. ASTYANAX DOUGLASS

Catcher Astyanax Douglass only played in eleven major league games, but he participated in one of baseball's greatest fights. On May 24, 1925, Douglass punched Philadelphia pitcher Jimmy Ring during a donnybrook on the field. The two men continued their fight in the clubhouse. Round three occurred at the train station that night.

7. JOHN L. SULLIVAN

John L. Sullivan was the heavyweight champion of the world from 1882 to 1892. A talented pitcher, he was offered a tryout by Cincinnati, but declined.

8. EDDIE MATHEWS

Eddie Mathews hit 512 home runs during his Hall of Fame career. The slugging third baseman also had the reputation of being one of the game's best boxers. He demonstrated his prowess in a 1960 game against Cincinnati. The Reds' Frank Robinson slid hard into third base. Mathews responded by flattening Frank, shutting his right eye. Robinson got his revenge by robbing Mathews of a home run later in the game.

9. BILL DICKEY

Yankees' catcher Bill Dickey threw one of baseball's most celebrated punches in a game against the Senators on July 4, 1932. Dickey broke the jaw of Washington outfielder Carl Reynolds after a close play at the plate. The fight precipitated one of the wildest brawls in baseball history. Dickey was suspended for thirty days.

10. NOLAN RYAN

Fans held their breath in 1993 when young Chicago third baseman Robin Ventura charged the mound to fight forty-six-year-old pitcher Nolan Ryan. Ryan grabbed Ventura in a headlock and planted six punches on his noggin.

The Bases Are Loaded

M any baseball greats were heavy drinkers: Grover Cleveland Alexander, Mickey Mantle, Hack Wilson, Ed Delahanty, King Kelly, and Rabbit Maranville, to name a few. In recent years, Dwight Gooden, Darryl Strawberry, and Bob Welch all sought treatment for their alcoholism. In 1989, reliever Mitch Williams was traded to Philadelphia. The Wild Thing wanted his old uniform number 28, which was being worn by John Kruk. Kruk agreed to relinquish his number in exchange for two cases of beer.

1. FLINT RHEM

St. Louis pitcher Flint Rhem led the National League with twenty wins in 1926. Rhem was scheduled to pitch a crucial game against Brooklyn in 1930 but failed to show up. Two days later, Rhem reappeared and claimed that he had been kidnapped by gamblers and forced to drink large amounts of whiskey to incapacitate him. Of course, Rhem had concocted the wild story after a drinking binge left him unable to pitch.

2. BUGS RAYMOND

Pitcher Bugs Raymond was such a chronic alcoholic that New York manager John McGraw hired a detective to keep tabs on him during his years with the Giants from 1909 to 1911. The surveillance ended when McGraw found Bugs and the detective in the midst of a drinking contest.

3. RUBE WADDELL

Rube Waddell had an ingenious ploy he used when he needed a drink. He had once outdueled the great Cy Young in a twenty-inning game. Waddell offered the game ball to a bartender for a drink. Bartenders all over the country proudly showcased the balls Waddell had given them.

Philadelphia owner Connie Mack devised a plan that he hoped would cure Rube of his drinking. Mack placed a worm in a glass of whiskey. As the worm wriggled and drowned, Mack asked Waddell if he understood the effects of drinking. Rube replied, "Yes, it means I won't get worms."

4. STEVE BILKO

Steve Bilko was a minor league sensation who never quite reached stardom in the majors, where he played from 1949 to 1962. Battling a weight problem, Bilko created a unique way to shed pounds. The first baseman had his bathtub filled with beer and ice. When hot water was poured on the mixture, Bilko had his own beer sauna. He sat on the toilet downing beers while sweating off the calories.

5. JOHNNY MIZE

Johnny Mize was known to enjoy a drink or two. In 1948, he finished a workout and went to take a shower. Giants' trainer Frank Bowman soaked his sweatshirt in alcohol. Bowman confronted Mize and asked if he had been drinking. When he denied it, Bowman lit the sweatshirt. Believing he had sweated alcohol during the workout, Mize swore he'd lay off the stuff.

6. RAY CALDWELL

New York manager Miller Huggins hired two detectives to tail alcoholic pitcher Ray Caldwell. When Caldwell joined the Indians, manager Tris Speaker had it written into his contract that he could only drink on the night after he pitched. The arrangement worked beautifully as Caldwell had his only twenty-game season in 1920.

7. TOAD RAMSEY

Toad Ramsey is credited with inventing the knuckleball. The pitch was so baffling that Ramsey won thirty-eight games in 1886 and struck out 499 batters. On July 25, 1888, Toad was arrested in Louisville for failing to pay a substantial overdue bar tab.

8. TOM SEATS

Tom Seats was a southpaw pitcher with great stuff but unsteady nerves. Brooklyn manager Leo Durocher discovered that if he gave Seats brandy before a game, he pitched well. Seats won ten games for the Dodgers in 1945, before General Manager Branch Rickey learned of the reason for his success and released the imbibing pitcher.

9. PAUL WANER

Pittsburgh outfielder Paul Waner had eight 200-hit seasons and a career batting average of .333. A hard drinker, Waner would sober up by doing from fifteen to twenty backflips before the game.

10. PRESIDENT HERBERT HOOVER

President Herbert Hoover attended Game three of the 1931 World Series between Philadelphia and

St. Louis. The country was in the depths of the Great Depression, and Hoover was not at the peak of his popularity. Baseball fans, unhappy after a decade of prohibition, chanted, "We want beer!" as the president left the ballpark.

Illegal Substances

The extent of the drug problem in baseball has become public in the last two decades. Dwight Gooden was on his way to becoming one of the greatest pitchers in baseball history until a problem with substance abuse derailed his career. Former Cy Young winner Vida Blue served three months in prison for possession of cocaine. Ex-Dodgers' outfielder Lou Johnson hocked his World Series ring to support his cocaine habit. Tim Raines kept a stash of cocaine in his hip pocket and slid headfirst to avoid damaging his drugs.

1. THE PITTSBURGH DRUG CONNECTION

The 1985 Pittsburgh drug trial exposed the widespread use of drugs by major league players. It became apparent that drug dealers had access to team clubhouses and that some players had been involved in not only the use of drugs but in their

Orlando Cepeda

Orlando Cepeda's election to the Hall of Fame may have been delayed because of a conviction for drug dealing.

distribution. Dave Parker, Keith Hernandez, Joaquin Andujar, Dale Berra, Jeff Leonard, Lonnie Smith, and Enos Cabell were suspended from baseball for one year by baseball commissioner Peter Ueberroth.

2. STEVE HOWE

Nobody has been given more second chances than pitcher Steve Howe. He was a talented young reliever for the Los Angeles Dodgers in the early 1980s when his problems with substance abuse began to surface. Howe was suspended for the entire 1984 season after testing positive for drugs. Between numerous drug rehabs, Howe has had stints with the Minnesota Twins, Texas Rangers, and New York Yankees.

3. LAMARR HOYT

LaMarr Hoyt led the American League in wins in 1982 and 1983. Hoyt started the All-Star Game in 1985, but the following year he won only eight games. Suspended for the 1987 season, Hoyt served forty-five days in jail for drug-related offenses. After a cache of cocaine and marijuana was discovered in his apartment, Hoyt was sentenced to a year in prison in 1988.

4. DOCK ELLIS

Dock Ellis was always controversial. In 1973, he showed up in a pregame workout wearing hair-curlers. Dock admitted he was under the influence of LSD when he no-hit the San Diego Padres on June 12, 1970. Ellis remembered very little of the game. He was high on drugs during much of his twelve-year career. "I was using everything," Ellis admitted.

5. ORLANDO CEPEDA

Orlando Cepeda was the Most Valuable Player in 1967 and belted 379 home runs during his career.

His reputation suffered when he was sentenced to prison in his native Puerto Rico for drug dealing. The scandal undoubtedly delayed his entry into the Hall of Fame. After being passed over by the baseball writers, Cepeda was finally selected by the veterans' committee in 1999.

6. PEDRO RAMOS

Pedro Ramos led the American League in losses four consecutive seasons from 1958 to 1961. His bad luck continued in 1979 when he was charged with drug trafficking and possession of cocaine. Ramos was sentenced to three years in prison.

7. PASCUAL PEREZ

Pascual Perez was a flamboyant pitcher who was 14–8 with Atlanta in 1984. A recurring drug problem culminated that year when he spent three months in prison in the Dominican Republic for possession of cocaine. The drug problem showed the next season when his record slipped to 1–13.

8. WILLIE AIKENS

Willie Mays Aikens was on top of the baseball world when he hit four home runs for the Kansas City Royals during the 1980 World Series. Aikens batted .302 and hit a career high of twenty-three home runs in 1983. That year Aikens was involved in a drug scandal in Kansas City and spent nearly three months in a federal prison. The first baseman's batting average plummeted nearly 100 points the next season. "I began to plan my day around when I was going to get high," Aikens confessed.

9. BLUE MOON ODOM

Pitcher John "Blue Moon" Odom was one of the stars of the championship Oakland A's teams of the early 1970s. Odom retired in 1976 and a decade later was convicted of selling cocaine.

10. FERRIS FAIN

Ferris "Burrhead" Fain was the American League batting champion in 1951 and 1952. In March 1988, authorities raided Fain's farm in California and confiscated over a million dollars worth of marijuana. The sixty-six-year-old farmer swore that he never inhaled and that his prize crop was grown strictly for profit.

You Can Bet on It

In the early days of professional baseball, gamblers frequented the ballparks. Large sums of money were bet on the games, and players were sometimes offered bribes. The term "hippodroming" referred to the practice of fixing games. The 1919 World Series was fixed by gamblers and numerous players, and owners have gambled or had associations with gambling ventures. Willie Mays and Mickey Mantle were banished from baseball for a time because they worked for casinos. New York Yankees' owner Del Webb had holdings in several Las Vegas casinos. After retirement, Hall of Fame pitcher Rube Marquard worked for several racetracks, and outfielder Elmer Flick occasionally drove harness horses. Reliever Rob Murphy started his own computerized business that assisted owners to select thoroughbreds by pedigree.

1. **PETE ROSE**

Pete Rose, baseball's all-time leader in hits and games played, was banned from baseball in 1989 because of his alleged betting on baseball. Rose was known to bet heavily on racehorses and associated with people with gambling interests. For years Charlie Hustle had been investigated by major league baseball. Although the commissioner's office indicated they had substantial proof that Rose bet on baseball, he always denied it. Commissioner Bart Giamatti banned Rose from baseball for life. Rose accepted the ruling as long as it was stipulated that there be no official finding that he bet on baseball. Giamatti seemed to violate the agreement when he concluded at the press conference that Rose had bet on baseball. Giamatti died of a heart attack a week later.

2. **WILLIAM COX**

Philadelphia Phillies' owner William Cox was forced to sell his team and was banned in 1943 because he had bet on baseball. His offense was to make around twenty small bets ($25 to $100) on the Phillies to win. He claimed that most of the wagers involved buying dinners or cigars. Cox said he didn't know betting on baseball was against the rules. Considering that the Phillies were one of the worst teams in baseball, betting on them should have been punishment enough.

3. CHARLES STONEHAM

William Cox was a small-time gambler compared to New York Giants' owner Charles Stoneham. He acquired the club in 1919, the same year as the Black Sox scandal. One of Stoneham's partners in a business venture was Arnold Rothstein, the professional gambler who was the man behind the World Series fix. Stoneham owned a racetrack and casino in Havana and had numerous suspicious connections that made him a less than ideal major league owner.

4. LEN DYKSTRA

On the field Len Dykstra was known for his aggressive play. "Nails" helped lead the 1986 New York Mets to the world championship and hit four home runs in the 1993 World Series for Philadelphia. In 1991, Dykstra admitted to losing $78,000 in high-stakes poker games.

5. ROGERS HORNSBY

Rogers Hornsby may have been the greatest righthanded batter in baseball history. His .358 career batting average is second only to Ty Cobb. The Rajah didn't drink or smoke, but he gambled excessively on horses. In 1927, a Cincinnati book-maker claimed that Hornsby owed him $92,000. The Kentucky Racing Commission notified Giants' owner Charles Stoneham that Hornsby owed them $70,000. Hornsby was never disciplined by the commissioner's office, although he was fired from a managerial position because of his betting.

6. DICK ALLEN

Dick Allen twice led the American League in home runs and was the Most Valuable Player in 1972. He admitted to losing large sums of money betting on and breeding thoroughbreds. Allen's brother, Hank, became a horse trainer after retiring from baseball. Dick Allen once said about Astroturf, "If horses can't eat it, I don't want to play on it."

7. ALBERT BELLE

Outfielder Albert Belle is one of baseball's most feared sluggers. On and off the field, Belle has been involved in numerous incidents, including allegedly trying to run over trick-or-treaters when they egged his house. Belle also admitted to los-ing as much as $40,000 betting on football, basket-ball, and golf matches. In 1997, he was interviewed in a federal investigation of bookmakers, although he was not the target of the probe.

8. **BOB RHOADS**

Bob Rhoads was a fine pitcher who won twenty-one games for Cleveland in 1906. One of baseball's great unsung heroes, he actually bailed out his team by gambling. The ballclub had run out of money on a preseason trip to Texas after two profitable weekend games in San Antonio were rained out. The owners needed $1,600 to pay hotel bills and purchase railroad tickets to Fort Worth where they were scheduled to play their next game. Bob Rhoads went to the Crystal Palace, a notorious gambling casino, and won $1,800 at the craps table. He gave the appreciative owners $1,600 and split the remaining $200 among the players.

9. **BRIAN MCRAE**

Friendly wagers are a part of any clubhouse. Cubs' outfielder Brian McRae bet weak-hitting pitcher Frank Castillo that he would never hit a home run in a game or batting practice. The stakes was a new Mercedes Benz. When Castillo connected for a homer in batting practice in 1997, McRae presented him with a $89,000 Mercedes Benz SL-320.

10. **DICK WAKEFIELD**

In one of baseball's dumbest wagers, Tigers' out-fielder Dick Wakefield bet Boston's Ted Williams $100 that he would outhit him in 1946. Not sur-prisingly, Williams won the bet, .342 to .268.

Out of Their Heads

Outfielder Jim Eisenreich was bothered early in his career from the effects of Tourette's Syndrome, a neurological disorder. Even great players such as Mickey Cochrane and Josh Gibson experienced nervous breakdowns. Over the years professional baseball players have endured everything from mental blocks to bouts of insanity. Losing is a daily occurrence in baseball. However, some players have actually lost their minds.

1. ED DOHENY

Ed Doheny was 16–8 for the Pittsburgh Pirates in 1903. Just prior to the 1903 World Series, Doheny went berserk in Boston and beat several men over the head with a poker. Paranoid, he believed the men were detectives sent to spy on him. Committed to a mental institution in Danvers, Massachusetts, Doheny assaulted a doctor with a cast iron stove footrest. He never played another major league game.

2. JIMMY PIERSALL

Jimmy Piersall's battle with mental illness often took place on the field for everyone to see. He swung back and forth in the dugout like a monkey. In Detroit he took a can of bug spray to the outfield. Another time, he did a hula dance in the outfield. When he hit his one hundredth career home run in 1963, Piersall ran around the bases backwards. After a mental breakdown, Jimmy Piersall received electroconvulsive shock treatments and had an eight-month period that was a complete blank. Despite insensitive fans who called him "wacko" and threw things at him, Piersall played seventeen seasons in the majors.

3. FRED PERRINE

Fred Perrine suffered sunstroke while umpiring a game in Cleveland in 1911. Perrine had a nervous breakdown and was committed to the Napa Asylum for the Insane. Two years later he committed suicide in an Oakland asylum.

4. PETE "THE GLADIATOR" BROWNING

Pete Browning was one of the great hitters of the nineteenth century. He played for four teams between 1882 and 1894. Browning was affected by

Jim Piersall
To celebrate his 100th major league home run in 1963, Jim Piersall ran around the bases backwards.

a mastoid infection that left him deaf. An alcoholic, Browning received poor medical treatment that caused brain damage. The Gladiator was committed to an insane asylum.

5. **RUBE FOSTER**

Rube Foster was an outstanding pitcher and a founder of the Negro Baseball League. Honus Wagner, who faced Foster in exhibition games, called him "one of the greatest pitchers of all time." In 1926, Foster began to display strange symptoms. He chased imaginary fly balls in the street. One of his saddest delusions was that he was going to pitch in the World Series. Foster spent the last four years of his life in a mental institution in Kankakee, Illinois.

6. JOHNNY EVERS

A series of tragedies led to the nervous breakdown of Chicago Cubs' second baseman Johnny Evers. He was driving when he had an accident in which his best friend was killed. Shortly thereafter, his business partner squandered his life savings. Evers's breakdown caused him to miss most of the 1911 season.

7. TONY HORTON

Tony Horton hit twenty-seven home runs for Cleveland in 1969. The next season the first baseman began to show signs of mental illness. On May 24, 1970, he blasted three home runs but was disturbed because the Indians lost when he failed to hit his fourth. A month later, he crawled back to the dugout after striking out on a blooper pitch thrown by Steve Hamilton. After the final out of a game, Horton went out to his position at first base. Manager Alvin Dark led him back to the dugout. Following the breakdown, Horton was given psychiatric help, during which he was not allowed to watch a baseball game on television.

Only twenty-five years old, he never played another game in the majors.

8. **ALEX JOHNSON**

Alex Johnson won the American League batting title in 1970. Johnson's nonchalance in the outfield made him constant trade bait. On a hot afternoon the outfielder positioned himself in the shadow of the foul pole. He threw a pop bottle at pitcher Clyde Wright and was fined a record twenty-nine times in less than half a season. Johnson's psychiatrist successfully argued before an arbitration panel that he was suffering from mental distress and should be entitled to disability pay.

9. **STEVE SAX**

Numerous players have experienced mental blocks of some sort. Perhaps the best known happened to second baseman Steve Sax. Early in his career with the Los Angeles Dodgers, Sax developed a phobia about throwing to first base. As his number of errors mounted, his career was in jeopardy. He tried everything to correct the problem, even putting socks over his eyes and throwing blindly to first base. Finally, in 1985 he was able to correct the problem by visualizing successful throws.

10. DR. HERNDON HARDING

The Los Angeles Dodgers had one of their worst
seasons in 1992, finishing the season with a 63–98
record. The team had psychiatrist Dr. Herndon
Harding travel with them to deal with the players'
mental distress over losing. Previously, the
Dodgers had called in hypnotist Arthur Ellen to
assist Maury Wills and Jerry Reuss with their performance. Ellen was able to help Reuss overcome
his fear of pitching in Chicago's Wrigley Field.

Overcoming Handicaps

These players overcame extraordinary physical handicaps to play in the major leagues.

1. PETE GRAY

In 1945, the defending American League champion St. Louis Browns called up a one-armed outfielder named Pete Gray. He had lost part of his arm at age six when he jumped from a moving truck. Batting one-handed, Gray hit .381 to win the batting title with Three Rivers of the American Canadian League. In 1944, he was voted the Most Valuable Player in the Southern League and stole home ten times. Promoted to the big leagues, Gray batted .218, remarkable considering his handicap. Fielding presented even a bigger problem. Gray had to field the ball, put his glove under his stump right arm, remove the ball, and throw. Runners sometimes were able to take an extra base. After a tough loss, an angry teammate challenged Gray to a fight with one of his arms tied behind his back.

2. HUGH DAILY

Hugh "One Arm" Daily had lost his left hand in a gun accident. Daily won twenty-five games in 1883 with Philadelphia of the National League. The following season he led the Union Association with an incredible 483 strikeouts, including nineteen in one game. Daily pitched back-to-back one-hitters in July 1884.

3. JIM ABBOTT

Jim Abbott was born without a right hand. Abbott starred at the University of Michigan before beginning a successful major league career mainly with California. The highlight of his career was pitching a no-hitter for the Yankees against the Cleveland Indians on September 4, 1993.

4. BERT SHEPARD

Former minor league pitcher Bert Shepard lost a leg when he was shot down over Germany during World War II. On August 14, 1945, Shepard, equipped with a wooden leg, allowed only one run in five innings, pitching for Washington against Boston. It was his only major league appearance.

5. DUMMY HOY

Despite being hearing-impaired, William "Dummy" Hoy had more than 2,000 base hits, scored more than 100 runs eight times, and stole 597 bases. An outstanding outfielder, Hoy set a record by throwing out three runners at the plate in a game on June 19, 1889. In 1886 during a minor league game, Hoy jumped on the back of a horse and made a spectacular catch. He was ninety-nine years old in 1961 when he threw out the first pitch in Game three of the 1961 World Series.

6. DUMMY TAYLOR

Deaf-mute Luther "Dummy" Taylor won twenty-one games for the New York Giants in 1904. Umpire Tim Hurst once ejected Taylor for cursing him out in sign language.

7. THREE FINGER BROWN

Mordecai "Three Finger" Brown used his handicap to become a Hall of Fame pitcher. Brown won twenty games six seasons in a row for the Chicago Cubs, and his career 2.06 earned run average is the third best in baseball history. A childhood accident with a corn shredder cost him part of his right index finger. He broke two fingers in a separate accident, leaving them gnarled. His deformed hand allowed him to grip the ball in such a way that he released pitches with an unusual spin. Brown won 239 games and lost only 129 in his fourteen-year career.

8. DAVE KEEFE

Dave Keefe lost his middle finger in a childhood accident. Keefe pitched in the major leagues from 1917 until 1922. He invented the fork ball, which he gripped between his second and fourth fingers. The pitch was later perfected by Pittsburgh reliever Elroy Face, whose forkball was so effective that he once won twenty-two consecutive games.

9. RED RUFFING

Between 1936 and 1939, New York Yankees' pitcher Red Ruffing won 20 games four consecutive seasons. He pitched twenty-two years in the majors and won 273 games. The Hall of Famer accomplished all this despite losing four toes on his left foot in a mining accident as a youth.

10. TOM SUNKEL AND JACK FRANKLIN

During World War II several handicapped players saw action in the major leagues. The old adage 'an eye for an eye' took on new meaning in 1944 when Brooklyn sent down virtually blind pitcher Tom Sunkel and promoted Jack Franklin who was blind in one eye.

Freak Injuries

Players have injured themselves in the most bizarre ways. St. Louis outfielder Vince Coleman got his leg caught in a mechanical tarp roller during the World Series. Five-time batting champion Wade Boggs injured his ribs taking off a pair of cowboy boots. Pitcher Orel Hershiser pulled a back muscle lifting his year-old son. Pitching prospect Steve Sparks dislocated his left shoulder attempting to tear apart a phone book in spring training. Cubs' outfielder José Cardenal missed opening day when his eyelid stuck shut. California pitcher Don Aase tore cartilage in his rib cage sneezing. Believe it or not, the following things actually happened.

1. RAY CALDWELL

Ray Caldwell pitched a no-hitter in 1919 and won twenty games for Cleveland the next season. In 1919, he was pitching a game in Philadelphia when an electrical storm blew in. Since there were two out in the ninth inning, umpires let play continue. A bolt of lightning struck Caldwell on the mound and knocked him cold for five minutes. When Caldwell was revived, he insisted on finishing the game. He did so with a flourish, striking out the final batter. Ray Caldwell was not the first major leaguer to be struck by lightning during a game. Five years earlier, New York outfielder Red Murray was hit while running the bases.

2. CREEPY CRESPI

Frank "Creepy" Crespi was a promising second baseman with the St. Louis Cardinals from 1938 to 1942. He entered the military service during World War II. In 1943, Crespi broke his left leg playing an army baseball game. While recuperating, he broke it again when he crashed into a wall during a wheelchair race. Crespi never played again in the major leagues.

3. BILLY MARTIN

Joe DiMaggio retired from baseball after the 1951 season. The following spring training, DiMaggio was working as a television commentator. He asked former teammate Billy Martin to demonstrate his sliding technique. Martin executed a perfect headfirst and hook slide. DiMaggio asked Martin if he would do a break slide. Martin slid too hard into the bag and broke his ankle.

4. JOE SPRINZ

Catcher Joe Sprinz played briefly in the major leagues with Cleveland and St. Louis from 1930 to 1933. On August 3, 1939, the veteran catcher was playing for the minor league San Francisco Seals when, as a publicity stunt, he attempted to catch a baseball dropped from a dirigible flying 1,000 feet above Treasure Island in San Francisco Bay. It hit him in the face, shattering his jaw and knocking out four teeth.

5. STEVE FOSTER

Pitcher Steve Foster was notified that he was being called up to the Cincinnati Reds in 1992. As Foster prepared to drive to the airport, he injured his shoulder throwing a suitcase onto his truck.

6. KEN HUNT

Rookie outfielder Ken Hunt hit twenty-five home runs for the Los Angeles Angels in 1961. In April 1962, he was flexing his back in the on-deck circle when he broke his collarbone. Hunt never batted above .185 in the majors again.

Ken Hunt
Angel's outfielder Ken Hunt had a promising career curtailed when he broke his collarbone while flexing his back in the on deck circle.

7. CHARLIE HOUGH

Knuckleballer Charlie Hough is one of the few pitchers to play twenty-five years in the major leagues. In spite of his endurance, Hough once broke a finger shaking hands with a friend.

8. JOE DIMAGGIO

In his much-anticipated major league debut in 1936, Joe DiMaggio injured his foot. The injury was made worse when he burned it during heat therapy. DiMaggio went on to hit 29 home runs and knock in 125 runs as a rookie.

9. DAVE KINGMAN

Dave Kingman hit 442 home runs and would have hit many more if he hadn't spent so much time on the disabled list. Kingman spent eleven days on the DL after injuring his knee while arguing a call with an umpire.

10. HOOKS WILTSE

Hooks Wiltse was a twenty-game winner for the New York Giants in 1908 and 1909. On July 4, 1908, Wiltse pitched a ten-inning no-hitter against Philadelphia. His most embarrassing moment came in 1905 when he was removed from a game because he swallowed his chewing tobacco.

The Big Hurt

B aseball can be a dangerous game. Occasionally it can even be fatal. Hall of Famer Hughie
Jennings was hit by pitches 260 times during his
career and suffered three skull fractures. California
pitcher Matt Keough underwent brain surgery in
1992 when he was hit by a line drive while sitting
in the dugout. Wee Willie Keeler once dove headfirst into a barbed wire fence making a catch and
was left hanging there.

1. RAY CHAPMAN

Ray Chapman is the only major leaguer to be
killed by a beaning. The Cleveland shortstop set
a major league record with sixty-seven sacrifices
in 1917 and the next year led the National League
in runs scored. On August 17, 1920, he was facing Carl Mays of the New York Yankees. Chapman
crowded the plate, and Mays had the reputation

of throwing high and tight. The sidearmer threw a pitch that sailed into the side of Chapman's head. The impact was so loud it could be heard throughout the Polo Grounds. Mays thought the ball had hit Chapman's bat and threw the ball to first base. Chapman, assisted by teammates, attempted to walk to the clubhouse in centerfield but collapsed. He died on the operating table the next day.

2. MIKE POWERS

Mike Powers was known as Hall of Famer Eddie Plank's personal catcher. The veteran was behind the plate on April 12, 1909, the first game played in Philadelphia's Shibe Park. In the seventh inning, Powers crashed into the wall while chasing a pop fly. Although he suffered internal injuries, Powers remained in the game. Hospitalized, he underwent three operations before dying two weeks later of gangrene of the bowel.

3. JOHNNY DODGE

Third baseman Johnny Dodge played two seasons in the major leagues with Philadelphia and Cincinnati. On June 18, 1916, Dodge was playing for Mobile in the Southern Association when he was beaned by Nashville's Shotgun Rogers. Dodge's skull was fractured, and he passed away the next day.

4. JESSIE BATTERSON

Nineteen-year-old Springfield third baseman Jessie Batterson was hit by a pitch thrown by Omaha's Swede Carlson in a game played on July 4, 1933. Batterson was able to walk to the clubhouse before collapsing. Carlson was at his bedside when he died following surgery.

5. OTTIS JOHNSON

Ottis Johnson died after being hit by a pitch made by Jack Clifton in an Alabama-Florida League game on June 2, 1951. Seemingly unaffected by the tragedy, Clifton pitched a no-hitter in his next start.

6. JAMES CREIGHTON

Perhaps the greatest player before the advent of the major leagues, James Creighton revolutionized pitching by being the first pitcher to change speeds and snap his wrist on his pitches. His hitting was so phenomenal that he once made only four outs during a season. He was only twenty-one years old in October 1862 when, playing for the Brooklyn Excelsiors, he ruptured his bladder hitting a home run. The admirable Creighton died four days later.

7. DON BLACK

The highlight of pitcher Don Black's career was a no-hitter he pitched against the Philadelphia A's on July 10, 1947. The next season the Cleveland pitcher took a hard swing at a pitch during a game against St. Louis. Black staggered away and collapsed behind home plate. He had suffered a brain hemorrhage and never played baseball again. Indians' owner Bill Veeck staged a benefit that raised $40,000 for the fallen pitcher.

8. MOOSE SOLTERS

Julius "Moose" Solters batted in more than 100 runs three consecutive seasons from 1935 to 1937. During a pregame warmup, the White Sox's outfielder waved to his brother-in-law in the stands. While Solters was looking at the stands, a ball thrown by another player hit him in the head. The freak injury caused Solters gradually to go blind.

9. LARRY BROWN

One of the worst collisions in baseball history took place on May 4, 1966 between Cleveland shortstop Larry Brown and outfielder Leon Wagner. Brown suffered fractures of the skull, nose, and cheekbone while Wagner's nose was broken. Brown recovered and played eight more seasons in the majors.

10. **PAUL BLAIR**

Paul Blair won eight gold gloves as an outfielder for the Baltimore Orioles. His career was nearly ended in 1970 when he was beaned by California pitcher Ken Tatum. Blair lay motionless with blood trickling out of his nose, mouth, and ears. Umpire Ron Luciano thought Blair was dead. Luciano wrote that Blair was never the same hitter, and he was never the same umpire. Blair underwent two years of hypnotherapy to help him overcome fear at the plate.

Cheaters Sometimes Win

Over the years players and managers have found ways to cheat. Hall of Fame pitcher Whitey Ford doctored the ball in almost every way imaginable. Jake Beckley hid a ball under the first base bag, which he used to tag out unsuspecting runners.

1. JOHN MCGRAW

As a member of the notorious Baltimore Orioles of the 1890s, third baseman John McGraw used almost every trick in the book to win. With only one umpire, players could get away with almost anything. Outfielders hid balls in the high grass. McGraw was notorious for tripping and obstructing runners. One of his favorite tricks was to put his finger in the belt loop of runners tagging up at third to keep them from getting a good jump.

2. CONNIE MACK

Connie Mack was only thrown out of one game in sixty-one years, yet the respected Mr. Mack wasn't above cheating to gain an advantage. He froze baseballs in order to make them travel less far when hit and sneaked them into the game when his pitchers were on the mound. Mack had a spy hidden in the centerfield scoreboard to steal the opposing team's signals.

3. MORGAN MURPHY

On September 17, 1900, Cincinnati was playing Philadelphia when the Reds' third base coach Tommy Corcoran uncovered a sign-stealing scheme employed by the home team. Corcoran's spikes caught in a wire in the coaches' box. He pulled up the wire and discovered that it was connected to the Phillies' locker room where catcher Morgan Murphy sat by a window with a telegraph. He had been stealing signals and sending them to the Phillies' third base coach. One buzz meant a fastball, two buzzes a curve, and three a change-up.

4. GAYLORD PERRY

Baseball's most notorious spitball pitcher, Gaylord Perry, won 314 games in his career and Cy Young Awards in both leagues. Perry went through a series of motions on the mound, touching his

Gaylord Perry
The secret to 300-game winner Gaylord Perry's super sinker was the foreign substances he had in his cap, jersey, belt, and pants.

glove, uniform, face, and bill of his cap before delivering a pitch. He hid foreign substances on parts of his body, cap, jersey, belt, and pants. Perry chewed gum or sea moss to keep his saliva flowing. When he threw his "super sinker," it was almost impossible to hit.

5. **ABNER DALRYMPLE**

Chicago outfielder Abner Dalrymple led the National League in hits, home runs, and runs at various times in his career. Dalrymple kept a ball concealed in his uniform. In 1880, he took away a home run from Boston's Ezra Sutton when the umpire lost track of the flight of the ball.

6. **EDDIE "THE BRAT" STANKY**

Leo Durocher said of Eddie Stanky, "He can't hit, can't run, can't field. He's no nice guy, but all he does is win." Stanky threw dirt in the eyes of baserunners trying to steal second. "The Brat" was adept at kicking the ball out of fielders' gloves. In 1977, Stanky quit after managing the Texas Rangers for one day because he couldn't stand the attitude of modern players.

7. **PREACHER ROE**

Elwin "Preacher" Roe attributed his success to the development of a spitball. When Roe was traded to Brooklyn in 1948, he began throwing a spitball. Preacher was 34–47 without the spitter and 95–37 with it. "I didn't sin against God," Preacher said of his use of the illegal pitch.

8. **NORM CASH**

Norm Cash won the batting title in 1961 with a .361 average. It was the only time in his seventeen-year career that he batted above .286. The Detroit first baseman admitted that he had used a loaded bat during his career year.

9. **HARRY STOVEY**

Harry Stovey led the league in home runs five times between 1880 and 1889. Through no fault of his own, the gentlemanly Stovey was given credit for a batting crown he didn't win. Manipulations by an official scorer who kept the statistics credited Stovey with a .404 batting average in 1884. A century later, researchers discovered that his real average was .326.

10. EDDIE AINSMITH

Eddie Ainsmith caught for the Washington Senators from 1910 until 1918. On a dark afternoon he was behind the plate when fireballing Walter Johnson was on the mound. With a two-strike count, Ainsmith popped his glove, and the umpire called strike three without Johnson ever delivering the ball.

Say It Ain't So, Joe

The banishment of Pete Rose in 1989 is the latest instance of an individual being placed on the permanently ineligible list. More than thirty men have been banned from baseball for various offenses. Here are ten:

1. **THE CHICAGO EIGHT**

Eight members of the Chicago White Sox were banned from baseball for life for throwing the 1919 World Series against Cincinnati. The players, resentful of low salaries they were paid by White Sox owner Charles Comiskey, agreed to throw games in exchange for payments from gamblers betting on the Reds. The banished players included Shoeless Joe Jackson, a lifetime .356 hitter, and pitcher Eddie Cicotte, a 210-game winner. Others banned included infielders Chick Gandil, Buck Weaver, Swede Risberg, and Fred McMullin, outfielder Happy Felsch, and pitcher

Lefty Williams. Weaver claimed he did not partici-
pate in the fix nor did he receive any money, but
he was banned by Commissioner Landis because
he knew about it and didn't tell anyone.

2. JIM DEVLIN

Jim Devlin won thirty games in both of his major
league seasons, and his 1.89 career earned run
average is the third best in baseball history. During the first two years of the National League, he
led pitchers in almost every significant category.
His Louisville Grays looked as though they were on
their way to the 1877 pennant when they lost several games suspiciously. After Louisville lost the
pennant to Boston, rumors began circulating that
the Grays had thrown games. Devlin, infielders Al
Nichols and Bill Craver, and outfielder George Hall
were banned for life. Players received as little as
$10 for their involvement in the scandal. Devlin,
who briefly was employed as a policeman, begged
for reinstatement until his death at age thirty-four
in 1883.

3. HAL CHASE

Slick-fielding first baseman Hal Chase won a batting title in 1916 and would probably be in the
Hall of Fame if he hadn't been one of the most
corrupt players ever to wear a uniform. Despite
his obvious defensive skills, Prince Hal led the

league in errors seven times. Although most of his managers suspected him of throwing games, he was so skillful that he managed to play fifteen years before he was unofficially blacklisted after the 1919 season. Reportedly, Chase won $40,000 betting on Cincinnati in the 1919 series. Following his banishment from the majors, Chase was also barred from the Pacific Coast League for involvement in a gambling ring and attempting to bribe an umpire.

4. RICHARD HIGHAM

Richard Higham has the dubious distinction of being the only major league umpire to be banished for life. In 1882, he was expelled for conspiring with gamblers to fix games.

5. HORACE FOGEL

The main reason that Philadelphia Phillies' owner Horace Fogel was banned for life was because he made unfounded charges that umpires made questionable calls to insure that the New York Giants won the 1912 pennant. Officially, he was banned for "undermining the integrity of the game."

6. HEINIE ZIMMERMAN

Heinie Zimmerman, the 1912 Triple Crown winner, was banished from baseball in 1919 for fixing games with his Giants' teammate Hal Chase.

7. BENNY KAUFF

Benny Kauff won the batting title in both years that the Federal League existed. In 1920, he was indicted for being part of an auto theft ring. Kauff owned a used car lot and was charged with receiving stolen property. Although he was acquitted in court, Commissioner Kenesaw Landis banned Kauff from baseball for life.

8. RAY FISHER

Ray Fisher won 100 games between 1910 and 1920 and pitched for Cincinnati in the 1919 World Series. He was banned from baseball in 1921 without a hearing or even an explanation. His offense was to accept the coaching position at the University of Michigan instead of signing a contract offered by the Cincinnati Reds. Fisher coached Michigan for thirty-eight years before being reinstated in the 1960s.

9. DUTCH LEONARD

Dutch Leonard threw two no-hitters, and his 1.01 earned run average in 1914 is the lowest in baseball history. He accused Ty Cobb and Tris Speaker, two of baseball's greatest stars, of fixing a game in 1919. Commissioner Landis dismissed the charges against Cobb and Speaker, but Leonard was banished for life for his involvement.

10. JOE GEDEON

Joe Gedeon is the least-known player banned because of the 1919 World Series. The St. Louis Browns' second baseman was banned for knowledge of the series fix. He was a close friend of Swede Risberg of the Black Sox.

Grand Slammers

Dozens of major leaguers have served time in jail or have had other run-ins with the law. Their crimes, or alleged crimes, have ranged from murders to misdemeanors.

1. LEN KOENECKE

Brooklyn outfielder Len Koenecke batted .320 in 1934, but he constantly broke curfews and ignored manager Casey Stengel's training rules. Stengel felt he was a bad influence on the team and sent Koenecke to the minors in September 1935. Koenecke got drunk and chartered a plane to Buffalo, where he had played in the minors. He attempted to take over the controls of the plane. During the struggle, pilot William Mulqueeny hit Koenecke over the head with a fire extinguisher. Mulqueeny was able to get the plane under control and made an emergency landing at a race track near Toronto. Len Koenecke, who had attempted history's first skyjacking, was dead.

2. JOHN GLENN

John Glenn played outfield and first base for Chicago in 1876 and 1877. In 1888, Glenn was accused of committing a robbery and raping a twelve-year-old girl. Glenn was accidentally shot and killed by a policeman who was trying to protect him from a mob.

3. DENNY MCLAIN

In 1985, former Tigers' pitcher Denny McLain was sentenced to twenty-three years in prison after being convicted on charges of racketeering, loan sharking, extortion, and possession of cocaine. After being released early, McLain was sentenced to eight years in prison for his involvement in a meatpackers' pension fund swindle.

4. PETE ROSE

In 1990, Pete Rose, baseball's all-time hit leader, pleaded guilty to two counts of filing false income tax returns. He failed to declare income of more than $354,000 on his 1985 and 1987 federal income tax returns. Rose spent five months in a federal prison in Marion, Illinois.

5. TURKEY MIKE DONLIN

The most popular player of his day, Turkey Mike Donlin batted .333 during his twelve-year career. In 1902, Donlin stalked Minnie Fields, an actress on whom he had a crush. Donlin assaulted her escort, Ernest Slayton, then hit the actress when she tried to intervene. Fields was knocked unconscious by the blow. For his crime, Donlin was sentenced to six months in jail and kicked out of the American League.

6. RON LEFLORE

Ron LeFlore was only twelve years old when he stole $1,500 from a grocery store. He spent a year in reform school when he was caught trying to crack a safe. He was nineteen years old in 1966 when he was arrested for armed robbery. LeFlore was sentenced to 5–15 years in prison. While serving his sentence at Jackson State Prison, he began playing baseball for the prison team. Inmates wrote Detroit manager Billy Martin raving about LeFlore's talent. In May 1973, Martin visited LeFlore in prison. A year after he was released, LeFlore made his major league debut. The outfielder played nine years in the majors and led both leagues in stolen bases.

7. JOE PEPITONE

Joe Pepitone was a colorful first baseman who played in the majors from 1962 until 1973. In 1985, Pepitone was pulled over by police officers in Brooklyn. Inside his automobile they discovered $70,000 worth of cocaine, heroin, and other illegal substances as well as a loaded gun. Pepitone served two months behind bars for the offenses.

8. KIRBY HIGBE

Brooklyn righthander Kirby Higbe led the National League with twenty-two wins in 1941. After his playing days were over, Higbe spent two months in jail in South Carolina for passing bad checks. He later worked as a prison guard.

9. BABE RUTH

On June 8, 1921, Babe Ruth was arrested for speeding in New York. Held in jail until midafternoon, he was permitted to change into his uniform in his cell. Given a police escort to Yankee Stadium, Ruth arrived in time to help the Yankees rally to a 4–3 victory.

10. DAVE WINFIELD

The New York Yankees were playing the Toronto Blue Jays on August 4, 1983, when outfielder Dave Winfield was arrested for a throw he made.

Between innings, he accidentally killed a seagull with a warm-up toss. Winfield killed two birds (the gull and the Jays) when he homered to give the Yankees a 3–1 victory. He was astonished to learn after the game that he was being arrested for cruelty to animals. The charges were dropped the next day.

Suicide Squeeze

Nearly 100 major league players and managers have committed suicide. They have killed themselves with guns, razors, strychnine, carbolic acid, carbon monoxide, and by hanging. Former outfielder Frank Bratchi ended his life in 1962 by drinking battery acid.

1. WILLARD HERSHBERGER

Cincinnati catcher Willard Hershberger is the only major leaguer to commit suicide during the season. In 1940 his Reds were contending for the National League pennant. Hershberger became despondent when he called for a pitch that the Giants' Harry Danning hit for a game-winning grand slam home run with two out in the ninth inning. Three days later, on August 3, Hershberger didn't come to the ballpark. When Hershberger's friend Dan Cohen was sent to check on him at the hotel, he found the catcher slumped in the bathtub. He had slashed his throat. Eleven years earlier, his father, ruined by the stock market crash, had sat on the rim of a bathtub and shot himself in the chest with a shotgun.

2. DONNIE MOORE

In 1985, Donnie Moore set an Angels' record with thirty-one saves and was voted the team's Most Valuable Player. The next season he saved twenty-one games despite pitching with a sore shoulder. More importantly, the Angels were in the playoffs. In Game five of the championship series against Boston, California led 5–2 going into the ninth inning. Leading three games to one, the Angels seemed on the verge of their first American League pennant. Moore was brought into the game with two outs in the ninth, a runner on first, and the Angels leading 5–4. Moore quietly got two strikes on batter Dave Henderson. He only needed one more strike. On a 2–2 pitch, Henderson hit a Moore delivery over the left-field fence to give the Red Sox the lead. The Angels tied the game in the bottom of the ninth, but Moore allowed the winning run in the eleventh inning. Boston won the next two games and the pennant. Moore said after the game, "I'll think about that until the day I die."

By 1988, arm miseries and a bone spur on his spine ended his career. On July 18, 1989, deeply in debt, with his marriage crumbling and his career over, Donnie Moore shot his wife, Tonya, three times. Rushed to the hospital by her daughter, she survived. With his ten-year-old son looking on, Moore, still haunted by the pitch that ruined his life, fatally shot himself.

3. ART IRWIN

Shortstop Art Irwin played thirteen seasons in the major leagues, finishing his career with Philadelphia in 1894. He is credited with being the first player to use a glove on a regular basis. On July 16, 1921, Irwin jumped overboard during a boat trip between New York and Boston. It was learned that he had been leading a double life. Irwin had one wife and family in Boston and another in Hartford.

4. CHICK STAHL

Outfielder Chick Stahl batted .358 as a rookie with Boston in 1897 and had a .307 career batting average. Late in the 1906 season, Stahl was named manager of a terrible Red Sox club that lost 105 games. He didn't want the responsibility and tried to resign in spring training the next year. Besides his doubts about being a manager, Stahl had plenty of problems off the field. His wife, Julia, was a drug addict and committed suicide a year after Stahl's death. In addition, another woman claimed she was pregnant with Stahl's child and threatened to make the news public if he didn't marry her. On March 29, 1907, Stahl committed suicide by drinking carbolic acid.

5. **WIN MERCER**

Chick Stahl was not the first newly appointed manager to take his own life. Five years earlier, Detroit skipper Win Mercer committed suicide by inhaling illuminating gas in a room at the Occidental Hotel in San Francisco on January 12, 1903. Mercer, who had lived up to his name by winning 131 games in the major leagues, left behind a suicide note warning of the evils of gambling and women. He was only twenty-eight years old.

6. **HARRY PULLIAM**

Pressure also contributed to the death of National League President Harry Pulliam in 1909. Pulliam had become league president in 1903 and led the senior circuit through an important transitional period, competing with the newly formed American League. His feud with Giants' manager John McGraw culminated with his ruling against New York in the celebrated Fred Merkle "bonehead" play. In February 1909, Pulliam had a nervous breakdown at the National League owners banquet. Five months later, on July 25, 1909, the thirty-nine-year-old Pulliam took off his clothes in his room in the New York Athletic Club and shot himself through the temple. Although the bullet had gone through his head and blown his right eye out, he was still conscious when help arrived, but he succumbed shortly thereafter. When McGraw learned of the tragedy, he joked, "I didn't think a bullet in the head could hurt him."

7. HUGH CASEY

Hugh Casey compiled a 75–42 record as a reliever with Brooklyn and three other teams between 1935 and 1949. He was notorious for his hard-drinking, womanizing lifestyle. Few players could drink as hard or fight as well. In July 1951, he called his estranged wife and threatened to blow his brains out if she didn't come back to him. When she refused, Casey kept his promise.

8. PEA RIDGE DAY

Clyde "Pea Ridge" Day would let out with a hog call when he struck out a batter. Unfortunately for him, it wasn't a common occurrence; he struck out forty-eight in four seasons in the majors. On March 21, 1934, Pea Ridge, Arkansas's most famous resident, depressed over an arm injury that curtailed his career, slit his throat with a hunting knife.

9. DANNY THOMAS

Outfielder Danny Thomas played two seasons with the Milwaukee Brewers. Devoutly religious, he refused to play ball on Sunday. On June 12, 1980, Thomas, accused of rape, committed suicide in a Mobile, Alabama, jail cell.

10. BRUCE GARDNER

Bruce Gardner was a pitching star in high school in the late 1950s. At age eighteen, he was offered a $66,000 bonus to sign with the Chicago White Sox. His coach advised him to complete his education at the University of Southern California. The advice proved unwise as Gardner received only a $12,000 bonus from the Dodgers upon graduation. A twenty-game winner in the minors, his dreams of a big league career were smashed by an arm injury. On June 7, 1971, he lay down on the pitching mound of the field where he played college ball. Clutching his college diploma, he fired a bullet through his head.

They Got Murdered

Since 1885, almost 40 major leaguers have been murdered. The players have been shot, stabbed, and even beaten to death with a baseball bat.

1. LYMAN BOSTOCK

Lyman Bostock was one of the finest young hitters of the late 1970s. The Twins' outfielder was second in the American League in batting in 1977 with a .336 average. The next year, Bostock went to the California Angels as a free agent. When he got off to a slow start, he asked owner Gene Autry to withhold his salary in April. By September, he was back near his usual .300. On September 23, he was riding in a car driven by his uncle in Gary, Indiana. Bostock was in the back seat with Barbara Turner, a woman he had just met. As the car stopped at an intersection, the woman's husband,

Leonard Turner, fired a shotgun blast through the back window. Bostock was hit in the head and died hours later.

2. ED MORRIS

Righthander Ed Morris won nineteen games as a rookie with the Boston Red Sox in 1928. On March 3, 1932, Morris was honored with a farewell fish fry in Century, Florida, on the eve of his departure for spring training. During the event, Morris got into an argument with a gas station owner, who then stabbed him to death.

3. LUKE EASTER

First baseman Luke Easter hit eighty-six home runs over a three-year period (1950–52) with the Cleveland Indians. He was employed as a bank messenger in Euclid, Ohio, in 1979 when he was the victim of a holdup. Easter was killed instantly by a blast from a shotgun.

4. EDDIE GAEDEL

Midget Eddie Gaedel gained baseball immortality in 1951 by coming to bat for the St. Louis Browns. Owner Bill Veeck took out a million dollar insurance policy on Gaedel to cover sudden death or sudden growth. While the latter never happened, the former did. In June 1961, Gaedel was mugged on a Chicago street. He managed to stagger home, where he died of a heart attack.

5. LARRY McLEAN

At 6 feet 5 inches and 230 pounds, catcher Larry McLean was a huge man for his time. He played thirteen seasons in the big leagues. Known for his drunken brawls, he was cut by the Giants in 1915 when he challenged manager John McGraw to a fight outside a St. Louis hotel. Six years later, McLean was engaged in a barroom brawl in Boston with another former player, Jack McCarthy, when the bartender shot him dead.

6. BUGS RAYMOND

One of the game's most notorious drunks, pitcher Bugs Raymond, was out of major league baseball by the time he was twenty-nine. A year later, on September 7, 1912, he was dispatched by a blow to the head with a baseball bat during a barroom brawl in Chicago.

7. FLEURY SULLIVAN

Twenty-two year old Fleury Sullivan lost thirty-five games for Pittsburgh of the American Association in 1884. It was his only season in the major leagues. On February 15, 1897, Sullivan was murdered in the midst of a heated political argument in East St. Louis, Illinois.

8. **ED IRVIN**

Ed Irvin was one of the replacement players used for one game in 1912 when the Detroit Tigers went on strike in support of the suspended Ty Cobb. The third baseman hit two triples in three at-bats but was never given another chance to play in the majors. On February 18, 1916, Irvin died when he was thrown through a saloon window in Philadelphia.

9. **PAT HYNES**

Pat Hynes appeared as an outfielder and pitcher for St. Louis in 1903 and 1904. On March 12, 1907, he went out drinking to celebrate his thirty-third birthday. That night he was shot and killed by a bartender in an argument over the bar tab.

10. **HI BITHORN**

Cubs' pitcher Hi Bithorn won eighteen games and led the National League with seven shutouts in 1942. A sore arm ended his major league stay in 1947. Bithorn tried to resurrect his career pitching in the Mexican Leagues. On New Year's Day, 1952, Bithorn was shot and killed in El Mante, Mexico, while trying to flee from police.

Murderers' Row

Murderers' Row is a term associated with the dangerous line-up of the 1927 New York Yankees. The line-up in this section consists of major league baseball players who committed murder.

1. MARTY BERGEN

Catcher Marty Bergen was depressed by the sudden death of his son in 1899. His erratic behavior troubled his Boston teammates, and they informed owner Arthur Soden that they wouldn't return if Bergen remained with the team. On January 19, 1900, Bergen used an ax and razor to murder his wife, six-year-old daughter, and three-year-old son before committing suicide.

2. TERRY LARKIN

Terry Larkin was a good enough pitcher to win thirty-one games for Chicago in 1879. Strangely he never won another game. After his retirement in 1884, Larkin went berserk, shot his wife, and cut his own throat. He and his wife survived. However, he was institutionalized and unsuccessfully attempted suicide again. Released, Larkin murdered his father-in-law, and on September 16, 1894, committed suicide with a razor.

3. **CHARLES SMITH AND FRANK HARRIS**

Charles "Pacer" Smith was a pitcher with Cincinnati during the first two seasons of the National League. Nearly twenty years later, he shot and killed his five-year-old daughter and teenage sister-in-law. On November 28, 1895, Smith was hanged at the Decatur, Illinois, prison, becoming the only major leaguer ever to be executed. A former teammate, catcher Frank Harris, was scheduled to be executed that same day on an unrelated murder charge, but he received a reprieve.

4. **CHARLIE SWEENEY**

Twenty-one-year-old pitcher Charlie Sweeney set a major league record when he struck out nineteen batters in a game on June 7, 1884. The record would last more than 100 years until Roger Clemens broke it in 1986. Sweeney won forty-one games in 1884 but was banned from the National League for walking off the field during a game. Washed up at age twenty-four, Sweeney murdered a man in a San Francisco saloon in 1894. He died in prison eight years later.

5. DANNY SHAY

Danny Shay was a major league shortstop during the first decade of the twentieth century. In 1917, Shay was involved in an argument with a waiter over the amount of sugar in a bowl on his table at an Indianapolis hotel. Shay pulled a gun and shot the man to death. Shay claimed self-defense and was acquitted, possibly because the victim was black.

6. HANK THOMPSON

Hank Thompson was the third African American to reach the major leagues, making his debut with the St. Louis Browns in 1947. During spring training in 1948, Thompson shot and killed a man in a bar who had pulled a knife on him. The shooting was ruled self-defense, and Thompson went on to star for the New York Giants between 1949 and 1956.

7. EDGAR MCNABB

Edgar McNabb was a rookie pitcher with the 1893 Baltimore Orioles. His mistress was a striking blonde actress named Laura Kellogg. After an argument in a Pittsburgh hotel room, McNabb shot Kellogg twice in the neck. Paralyzed, Kellogg would later die from the wounds. On February 28, 1894, McNabb fatally shot himself in the mouth.

8. CESAR CEDENO

When Cesar Cedeno came up with Houston in 1970, he was touted as the "next Willie Mays." When he hit .320 in 1972 and 1973, he appeared to be fulfilling his promise. On December 11, 1973, Cedeno was spending the night with his nineteen-year-old mistress at a motel in Santo Domingo. During the night, the woman, Altragracia de la Cruz, was shot in the head and killed during an apparent struggle for Cedeno's gun. Cedeno claimed it was an accident and was found guilty of involuntary manslaughter. The punishment turned out to be a 100-peso fine. Cedeno played in the majors until 1986, but he never reached his Hall of Fame potential.

9. PINKY HIGGINS

Pinky Higgins was a hard-hitting third baseman who played in the majors from 1930 to 1946. In 1938, he set a major league record with twelve consecutive base hits. Higgins was convicted of vehicular homicide after he struck and killed a highway worker in 1968. Paroled after serving two months, he died of a heart attack the day after his release.

10. **ART SHIRES**

Art "The Great" Shires's four-year baseball career was overshadowed by his violent behavior. When he wasn't fighting professionally, he kept in shape by beating up players and managers. In 1928, he nearly killed a black fan in Waco, Texas, when he hit him with a baseball. Twenty years later, he was charged with murder during a fight with an old friend. Shires confessed, "I had to rough him up a good deal because he grabbed a knife and started whittling on my legs." At his trial he was acquitted because of testimony that death had been caused by cirrhosis of the liver, and the beating itself wouldn't have been fatal.

Baseball's Greatest Mysteries

M any fans wonder why the Cubs or Red Sox never win a championship. Let's conclude this book by contemplating some of baseball's unsolved mysteries.

1. WHO INVENTED BASEBALL?

The myth that Abner Doubleday invented baseball in Cooperstown, New York, in 1839, originated in 1907. A commission, headed by A. G. Spalding, had convened to determine the origins of the national pastime. An elderly man named Abner Graves claimed that he had been present at the first game in Cooperstown. When the Baseball Hall of Fame was built thirty years later, Cooperstown was selected as the site. Over the years, researchers have concluded that the Doubleday story is completely false. There is no evidence that Doubleday, who later gained fame as a union general in the Civil War, visited Cooperstown in 1839. Doubleday kept sixty-seven diaries in his lifetime, none of which even mentions baseball. More significantly, there are references to a game resembling baseball being played in America as early as the eighteenth century. In all likelihood, the game evolved from English games such as rounders and town ball. During the Cold War, the Russians even suggested that our national pastime had been copied from their game, lapta. A bizarre footnote occurred in 1924 when ninety-year-old Abner Graves, the man who concocted the Doubleday myth, murdered his wife and was committed to an institution for the criminally insane.

2. WHO INVENTED THE CURVE?

Candy Cummings won only twenty-one games, but he was one of the first inductees into the Baseball Hall of Fame because he claimed to have invented the curve ball. Cummings wrote that he got the inspiration for the pitch while throwing clam shells as a teenager in 1863. He threw his first curve in competition in 1867. A number of other pitchers claimed to be the pitch's originator. Alphonse Martin said he had been throwing the dropball since 1864. Fred Goldsmith claimed that he had invented the pitch in the mid-1860s. In

1870, he made headlines by demonstrating that the ball really curved. Previously, many thought the movement was just an optical illusion. Bitter over his lack of recognition, Goldsmith died in 1939 clutching the sixty-nine-year-old newspaper account of his demonstration. That same year Candy Cummings was inducted into the Hall of Fame.

3. TY COBB AND TRIS SPEAKER

Two legends of the game, Ty Cobb and Tris Speaker, probably fixed a game in September 1919. In 1926, Detroit pitcher Dutch Leonard revealed that he and Cobb met with Speaker and Smokey Joe Wood of the Indians to discuss fixing a game so that Detroit would finish third. The men also agreed to bet on the Tigers. Detroit won 9–5, but Cobb and Speaker were unable to get their bets down. Leonard revealed the fix in 1926, after Cobb demoted him to the minor leagues. As proof, he presented letters he had received from Cobb and Wood detailing the plot. Detroit owner Frank Nevin and American League President Ben Johnson, eager to keep the scandal out of the headlines, bought the letters for $20,000. When Commissioner Kenesaw Landis learned of the fix, he investigated the matter. Although he had banned numerous lesser players for similar offenses,

Landis allegedly decided it was not in the best interest of baseball to banish Cobb and Speaker. They did resign as managers, and both ended their careers as part-time players on the 1928 Philadelphia Athletics.

4. PETE ROSE

Pete Rose was banned from baseball in 1989 by Commissioner Bart Giamatti for allegedly betting on baseball. Rose has always denied the charge. However, there would appear to be substantial evidence that he not only bet on baseball, but that he wagered on games he was managing. At least nine of Rose's associates interviewed by the commissioner's office testified that he bet on baseball. They produced betting sheets in Rose's handwriting. Investigator John Dowd wrote a 225-page report that concluded that Rose bet thousands of dollars daily on baseball games and that he bet repeatedly on the Cincinnati Reds, the team he was managing. There is no evidence that he ever bet against the Reds, although Paul Janszen, one of Rose's cronies, claimed he would consider betting against them if the money was right. It must be noted the Giamatti appeared to already have his mind made up before all the evidence was in. It seemed more a battle of wills than a matter of principle. One of baseball's great players was banned from baseball and kept out of the Hall of Fame. Giamatti died of a heart attack a week after his ruling. Nobody really won.

5. **ED DELAHANTY**

Ed Delahanty's .346 lifetime batting average is the fifth best in baseball history. Big Ed was batting .333 in June 1903 when he was suspended for excessive drinking. On July 2, he was on a train bound for New York when he became rowdy. The conductor threw the drunken Delahanty off the train in Fort Erie, on the Canadian side of the Niagara River. Railroad workers testified that they had seen Delahanty chasing the train on foot across the railroad bridge. He apparently fell to his death, and his body was washed over Niagara Falls. Probably his death was accidental. However, some believe he committed suicide because he had recently taken out a large insurance policy with his daughter as his beneficiary. Others believe that because he was carrying valuable jewelry, and the diamonds were never found, that he might have been murdered.

6. **DON WILSON**

Houston pitcher Don Wilson threw no-hitters in 1967 and 1969. He was denied a chance at a third in September 1974, when manager Preston

Gomez removed him for a pinch-hitter in the ninth inning. On January 5, 1975, Wilson was found dead in his car, which was parked in the garage of his home. He had died from carbon monoxide poisoning. His five-year-old son, sleeping in his bedroom, also died. Although many believed Wilson committed suicide, his death was ruled accidental.

7. WHO WAS CASEY?

Ernest Thayer published his poem, "Casey at the Bat" in 1888. Although he insisted to his dying day that the mighty Casey was a completely fictional character, others have made claims that they were the inspiration for the character. Some think it was King Kelly, the most popular player of the time. Dan Casey and his brother Dennis, both active major leaguers in the 1880s, also laid claim, if for no other reason than because they shared the same name. It didn't seem to matter that Dan Casey was a pitcher. Why anyone would want to be the inspiration for a character who struck out and lost a game is an even greater mystery.

8. BILL THOMAS

Bill Thomas was a promising young pitcher in the Pacific Coast League. In April 1906, Thomas boarded a boat, the *Richard Peck,* headed for

New York. The night before the boat was to arrive in New York he instructed the porter to get him up early because he wanted to see the sunrise over the city. When the man entered Thomas's room, he found his bed empty. Thomas was never seen again. Whether he jumped or fell overboard or was the victim of foul play remains a mystery.

9. **RUBE WADDELL**

Before the 1905 World Series, gamblers offered Philadelphia ace Rube Waddell $17,000 not to play in the World Series. Waddell had led the American League with twenty-six victories, and his participation was essential if the A's were going to defeat the heavily favored New York Giants. Just prior to the series opener, Waddell claimed he hurt his pitching arm falling over a suitcase. Without Waddell, the A's won only one game in the series.

It was rumored that Waddell did make the deal with the gamblers, but he was cheated out of all but $500 of the bribe. Philadelphia owner Connie Mack insisted that Waddell was injured horsing around at the train station with teammate Andy Coakley. Whatever the truth, Waddell missed his only opportunity to pitch in the World Series. Another piece of evidence that would substantiate his claim of injury was that he never won twenty games again.

10. **STEVE BLASS**

One of the great mysteries of baseball is the sudden unexplained decline of Pittsburgh starter Steve Blass. From 1964 to 1972, Blass had won 100 games and lost 67. In 1972, he was 19–8 with a 2.49 earned run average. The next season he couldn't get the ball over the plate or anybody out. He walked eighty-four batters in eighty-eight innings. The previous season he had walked the same number of batters in 250 innings. His record slipped to 3–9, and his earned run average ballooned to 9.85. No advice from the pitching coach seemed to help. The trainers found nothing wrong with him physically. He tried everything: psychotherapy, hypnosis, visualization, and even meditation, but nothing worked. Perhaps Blass had experienced a mental block. The 1972 Pirates had lost the playoffs to Cincinnati in a heartbreaking ninth inning rally. Whatever the cause, no remedy was ever found, and Blass was out of baseball by 1974.

Bibliography

Berlage, Gai. *Women in Baseball.* New York: Praeger, 1994.

Blake, Mike. *Bad Hops and Lucky Bounces.* Cincinnati: Betterway Books, 1995.

Carter, Craig. *The Complete Baseball Record Book.* St. Louis: Sporting News, 1987.

Charlton, James. *The Baseball Chronology.* New York: Macmillan, 1991.

Conner, Floyd, and John Snyder. *Day By Day in Cincinnati Reds History.* New York: Leisure, 1983.

Dewey, Donald, and Nicholas Acocella. *The Biographical History of Baseball.* New York: Carroll & Graf, 1995.

Fusselle, Warner. *Baseball... A Laughing Matter.* St. Louis: Sporting News, 1987.

Gregorich, Barbara. *Women at Play.* New York: Harcourt Brace, 1993.

Gutman, Dan. *Baseball Babylon.* New York: Penguin, 1992.

Hoppel, Joe, and Craig Carter. *The Sporting News Baseball Trivia Book.* St. Louis: Sporting News, 1983.

James, Bill. *The Bill James Historical Abstract.* New York: Villard, 1986.

Kaufman, Alan, and James Kaufman. *The Worst Pitchers of All Time.* Jefferson (N. C.): McFarland, 1993.

Liss, Howard. *More Strange But True Sports Stories.* New York: Random House, 1981.

Marazzi, Rich, and Len Fiorito. *Aaron to Zipfel.* New York: Avon, 1985.

Nash, Bruce, and Allan Zullo. *The Baseball Hall of Shame.* New York: Pocket Books, 1985.

————. *The Baseball Hall of Shame II.* New York: Pocket Books, 1986.

————. *The Baseball Hall of Shame III.* New York: Pocket Books, 1987.

————. *The Baseball Hall of Shame IV.* New York: Pocket Books, 1990.

————. *Baseball Hall of Shame's Warped Record Book.* New York: Collier, 1991.

Nelson, Kevin. *Baseball's Greatest Insults.* New York: Fireside, 1984.

Nemec, David. *Great Baseball Feats, Facts, & Firsts.* New York: Plume, 1987.

Peary, Danny. *Cult Baseball Players.* New York: Fireside, 1990.

Porter, David. *Biographical Dictionary of American Sports: Baseball.* Westport (Ct.): Greenwood Press, 1987.

Reichler, Joseph. *The Baseball Encyclopedia.* New York: Macmillan, 1988.

Scheinen, Richard. *Field of Screams.* New York: Norton, 1994.

Shalin, Bruce. *Oddballs.* New York: Penguin, 1989.

Shatzin, Mike. *The Ballplayers.* New York: Arbor House, 1990.

Snyder, John. *Play Ball*. San Francisco: Chronicle, 1991.

———. *World Series*. San Francisco: Chronicle, 1995.

Thorn, John, and John Holway. *The Pitcher*. New York: Prentice Hall, 1987.

Thorn, John, and Pete Palmer. *Total Baseball*. New York: Warner, 1989.

Weiss, Peter. *Baseball's All Time Goats*. Holbrook (Mass.): Adams, 1992.

Index

About the Author

Floyd Conner is a lifelong baseball fan and the author of ten books. His sports books include *Golf!*, *Fore!*, and *This Date in Sports History.* He also co-authored *Day By Day in Cincinnati Reds History* and the best-selling *365 Sports Facts a Year Calendar.* He lives in Cincinnati with his wife, Susan, and son, Travis.